MIGRATION OF HMONG TO THE MIDWESTERN UNITED STATES

Cathleen Jo Faruque

University Press of America,® Inc.
Lanham · New York · Oxford

Copyright © 2002 by
University Press of America,® Inc.
4501 Forbes Boulevard
Suite 200
Lanham, Maryland 20706
UPA Acquisitions Department (301) 459-3366

PO Box 317
Oxford
OX2 9RU, UK

Library of Congress Cataloging-in-Publication Data

Faruque, Cathleen Jo.
Migration of Hmong to the midwestern United States /
Cathleen Jo Faruque.
p.   cm
Includes bibliographical references and indexes.
1. Hmong Americans—Middle West—Social conditions. 2. Hmong
Americans—Middle West—Ethnic identity. 3. Hmong Americans—
Cultural assimilation—Middle West. 4. Immigrants—Middle West—
Social conditions. 5. Hmong (Asian people)—Migrations. 6. Middle
West—Social conditions. 7. Middle West—Ethnic relations.
8. Middle West—Emigration and immigration. 9. Asia,
Southeastern—Emigration and immigration. I. Title.
F358.2.H55 F37   2002
305.895'942077—dc21   2002035822 CIP

ISBN 0-7618-2443-X (paperback : alk. ppr.)

Dedication

In Memory of my Mother
Lorraine N. Cieminski
July 20, 1934 to May 22, 1998.
I only wish she was able to see this day,
for her belief in my abilities never wavered.

Contents

Foreword

In this text, *Migration of Hmong to the Midwestern United States,* Dr. Cathleen Jo Faruque provides much needed research and empirical information about Hmong refugees and their acculturation needs.

The decades following the 1960s have seen steady increases in the number of immigrants entering the United States of America. This trend peaked in the 1990s with what many demographers believe was the greatest wave of immigration in America's history; in the 1990 census, nearly 20 million foreign born people were counted. Quite significantly, recent immigrants have not only located in major urban areas such as Los Angeles, New York, Miami, Chicago, Houston, and San Francisco, but they have also located in suburbs and smaller cities across the United States. These trends make it imperative that psychologists, therapists, and human service professionals have access to research that helps them to understand the many facets of diversity and helps them to develop services and treatment modalities that are specifically responsive to diverse ethnic and racial groups, such as the Hmong who are the subject of this research study.

Approximately 300,000 Hmong have migrated to the United States of America, primarily to escape political persecution in China, Laos, Thailand, and Vietnam. The largest populations of Hmong refugees are located in California, Minnesota, and Wisconsin. As of 1998, an estimated 50,000 Hmong live in Minnesota. Although the Hmong have migrated to the United States in large numbers over the past 20 years, prior to this text, little in-depth research had been undertaken to examine the diversity and uniqueness of the Hmong people. Without research, services provided for the Hmong tend to be sparse, fragmented, and generally ineffectual.

From Dr. Faruque's study of a small population of Hmong living in Rochester, Minnesota, this text offers an in-depth analysis of the unique adaptation problems and needs of the Hmong people located in the Midwestern United States. The study examines the following primary

vii

aspects:

1. The effect non-voluntary migration has on the acculturation levels as measured by cultural awareness and ethnic loyalty of the Hmong in Rochester, Minnesota.
2. How the Hmong perceive the host Anglo-culture.
3. How the Hmong adjust to their host social system in the United States.
4. How much the Hmong learn from their new environment.
5. How the Hmong retain traditions within the United States.

Dr. Faruque's conclusions are enlightening, and she offers significant recommendations for further study of the Hmong refugees. The research study presented in this text is a valuable addition of the body of literature on the subject of Hmong immigration to the United States; it provides a base of knowledge needed for responding to the needs of the Hmong people and for empowering them to become active participants in the greater community.

Hosea L. Perry
Professor Emeritus
Department of Sociology and Social Work
Winona State University
Winona, Minnesota

Preface

This book was designed to stimulate interest in the helping profession of the utility of qualitative research in transcultural practice. This book was designed to investigate one of the newest refugee groups to the Midwestern United States, the Hmong refugees from Laos, China, Vietnam and Thailand.

This book examines how multigenerational Hmong families are adjusting and adapting to life in Rochester, Minnesota. The following questions guided the qualitative research presented in this text: (1) What effect does non-voluntary migration have on the acculturation levels as measured by cultural awareness and ethnic loyalty of the Hmong in Rochester, Minnesota? (2) How do the Hmong perceive their host Anglo culture? (3) How do the Hmong adjust to their host social system in the United States? (4) How much do Hmong learn about their new environment? (5) How do the Hmong retain traditions within in the United States?

Qualitative interviewing through in-depth individual interviews and participant observation was the method of data collection. Participants were recruited through purposive sampling, volunteering, and snowball sampling techniques. Criteria for inclusion in this study were: 1) Being Hmong; 2) Residing in Rochester, Minnesota, and; 3) Being between at least 13 years of age or older. Grounded theory methodology was the primary tool of data analysis.

In this book the reader will find that the Hmong subjects interviewed for this study showed a high degree of discrepancy between the acculturation levels based on age and country of origin from point of migration. This discrepancy has created an acculturation gap which is related to the younger Hmong's increased identification with the American culture and their decreased identification with their family's culture of origin. This shift has created family difficulties and communication gaps between family members.

Acknowledgments

To the numerous friends and colleagues who provided support, encouragement and guidance along the way, I send my sincere thanks. To Lee Chang and his father, Youa Kao Chang, words cannot express the support and assistance you provided in this project. Without your help, this textbook would have never happened. I also wish to thank Toulee Moua and Mike Lee for their interest in this study and the extra time they spent with me answering questions and clarifying different aspects of the Hmong culture. Hosea Perry, Winona State University Professor, retired, who painstakingly reviewed my work, provided feedback, guidance and support, I am truly grateful.

To my friends and colleagues at Winona State University, thank you. Special thanks go to Dr. Peter Henderson, for his belief and support of my work. To Winona State University's Department of Sociology and the Social Work Program, from faculty to staff who were supportive and helpful. Especially to Dr. Ruth Charles, for the many helpful suggestions and times she made available to discuss the nuances of qualitative research, Dr. John Collins and Ellen Holmgren, who patiently listened when I needed it.

I also wish to acknowledge the support of my family members: My father, Richard J. Cieminski, my sister, Nancy A. Cieminski, my brother-in-law, Mark R. Kalmes, my Uncles Richard Gora and Ed Kinsler, my brother, R.J. Cieminski, and my sisters Constance Wagner and Judith Weiland. Without their understanding and encouragement I am sure this would not be a finished work today.

I am also deeply appreciative of my dear husband, Syed M. Faruque who provides his insight, wisdom, patience, and strength every day.

Chapter 1

Coming to America

The 1990's saw one of the largest waves of immigration ever seen in the history of the United States of America. Many demographers believe that the 1990's saw more new immigrants entering the United States than any other decade in the history of America. Unique to our modern times, the United States of America has become a refuge for immigrants from developing countries in massive proportions since the 1960's.

The number of foreign born people residing in the United States is currently at an all time high with over thirty million foreign born persons counted in the 2000 census (U.S. Census, 2000). Recent immigrants have left a significant impact because of their choices to relocate in eight highly urban areas. These urban cities are: Los Angeles, New York City, Miami, Anaheim, Chicago, Washington D.C., Houston, and San Francisco (Koltyk, 1998).

For many decades, the larger cities were the main locations for persons from different cultures and as a result, were quite visible to the larger population. However, in more recent years, American suburbs, smaller cities, villages, and towns are hardly the homogeneous communities that were once portrayed in popular American literature. Psychologists, therapists, social workers, and other persons in the helping professions everywhere are now being challenged to develop services and diverse treatment modalities that are more representative, responsive, and relevant to multi-ethnic groups, persons of color, religious, and varied sexual oriented groups.

The reasons immigrants make the conscious decision to migrate to the United States are as diverse as the very people who come here. An immigrant family's dreams and fears about immigration become a unique and integral part of the family's cultural heritage.

Refugees, like the Hmong, who fled political persecution and severe trauma from a long waged war and its considerable devastation see little to no possibility of ever returning to their homeland. These people frequently experience the greatest difficulties in adapting to life in a new country, even more so than those who have come seeking economic opportunity and carrying a dream of one day being able to return to their homeland with a considerable savings.

Immigration to the United States of America has different meanings to the varied people who make the decision to migrate. Immigration frequently means increased opportunities for professional and economic growth, reunification with family members and loved ones who left the homeland some time before, freedom from political persecution and the opportunity to express one's religious beliefs freely. For many who chose to migrate, the unexpected consequences that provide significant challenges are dealing with ethnic bias, racial prejudice and stereotyping, language barriers, and loss of family and loved ones that were left behind. All migrants face new social rules and norms, which leave many with their most basic beliefs and values challenged or questioned. Customs and behaviors that may have served a person well in his or her country of origin, may not be so easily accepted or embraced by the host society. All migrant families face having to learn about a new culture, how to handle conflicts between the host culture and one's culture of origin, and transitioning or functioning effectively in a new and strange environment.

The Refugee Act of 1980, classifies a person as a refugee when he or she is unable to return to his or her country of origin because of persecution or the well-founded fear of persecution due to one's race, religion, nationality, membership in a particular group considered a minority to the homeland, or for political reasons. Immigrants are distinguishable from refugees by the very fact that immigrants make a voluntary and conscious decision to migrate (Haines, 1996).

The pre-migration experience of a refugee uniquely differs from those of many immigrants, especially when considering the nature of the refugee's departure from his or her home country and the length of time that was spent in refugee camps before resettlement. In the case of the Hmong refugees, escape from Laos and Vietnam was very traumatic and even quite dangerous. Long stays in refugee camps, predominately in Thailand, were marked by severe and over-crowded conditions, deprivation of food and sanitary drinking water, as well as basic necessities for survival. The time spent in these refugee camps were a significant and meaningful part of the Hmong pre-migration experience.

A major policy concern of refugees is the initial resettlement period and the adjustment time necessary to adapt to the new host environment. Further it is important to note the refugee's capacity to achieve economic self-sufficiency after an appropriate period of adjustment (Strand and Woodrow, 1985).

Each of us experiences a cultural system that dictates the rules for certain and expected behaviors, values, and beliefs. Enculturation is the natural and often unconscious process by which people acquire their own set of cultural beliefs and values. The United States of America is home to hundreds of different ethnic groups, each in and of itself a distinct and unique cultural system. Through the process of acculturation, the pure native cultural system of a group is slowly and inevitable lost, thus producing a merging and mingling of the old and new cultures, making them, after a period of years, indistinguishable from each other.

When migrants to the United States experience acculturation, they adopt a second set of cultural rules and norms. This second set of rules and norms will ultimately coexist with the rules and norms of their native culture, replace those of the old culture, or modify them so that the two sets actually complement each other. Few migrants are truly bicultural, but many retain the use of two sets of rules and norms from different cultures simultaneously (Koltyk, 1998).

The Framework

A Statement of the Research Problem

The purpose of the research and this book is to present to the reader the investigation of one of the more recent refugee groups to arrive in the Midwestern United States. This research was conducted on the Hmong people who were refugees from Laos, China, Vietnam and Thailand. This book examines how multigenerational Hmong families have adjusted to life in the city of Rochester, Minnesota.

The primary research question which precepitated and served as a guide to this study: *What affect does non-voluntary migration have on the acculturation levels as measured by cultural awareness and ethnic loyalty of the Hmong people residing in Rochester, Minnesota?* Specific to this research question, the following further questions were explored: *How do Hmong people perceive their host Anglo culture? How do the Hmong adjust to their host social system in the United States? How much do the Hmong know about their host culture? To what extent do the Hmong retain their own cultural traditions within the United States?*

Definition of Terms

The following terms are used interchangeably throughout this book. The description of meaning is intended to familiarize the reader with how these terms are used within the context of this study.

Acculturation: A process by which continuos contact between two or more distinct societies cause cultural change. The beliefs and customs of the two groups sometimes will merge almost equally and result in a single or "new" culture. More often, however, one society completely absorbs the cultural patterns of another. This change can frequently occur because of political or military domination (Encarta On-Line, 1999).

Adaptation: An individual's capacity to adapt to the surrounding new environmental conditions. Adaptation implies that a person must make change or must adjust to the new conditions or environment in order to continue with effective functioning (Zastrow and Kirst-Asham, 1994).

Anglo-American: The cultural identity of North Americans whose common spoken language is English and whose beliefs and customs historically come from areas predominantly in Northern Europe. Anglo-Americans are comprised of persons from the United States and Canada, with the French speaking Canadian a notable exception to the rule (Encyclopedia Britannica, 1999).

Assimilation: The process by which an individual or a group is absorbed into the dominant society. Assimilation usually involves a gradual change and takes place in varied degrees. Full assimilation occurs when a newer member of society becomes indistinguishable from other older and more established members (Encarta On-Line, 1999).

Culture: The beliefs, behaviors, language, and the entire way of life of a particular time, place, and group of people. Culture includes customs, ceremonies, traditions, inventions, technology, and works of art (Encarta On-Line, 1999).

Enculturation: An often natural and unconscious process by which people develop and acquire cultural beliefs (Koltyk, 1998).

Ethnicity: An ethnic group or a segment of a larger society whose members are thought, by themselves and perhaps by others, to have a common origin. These members share important segments of a common culture and participate in shared activities in which the culture, origin, values, and beliefs are significant components (Hein, 1997).

Hmong: Also referred to a Meo, these are a mountain-dwelling people of Chia, Vietnam, Laos, and Thailand. Their language heralds from Sino-Tibetan dialetics (Encyclopedia Britannica, 1999).

Migration: The permanent change of residence by an individual or group; it excludes such movements as nomadism, migrant labor commuting, and tourism, which are transitory in nature (Encyclopedia Britannica, 1999).

Refugee: A person who has fled or been expelled from his or her own country of origin because of natural catastophe, war, or military occupation, fear of religious, political, or racial persecution (Encarta On-Line, 1999).

A Brief Review of the Literature

The United States of America has increasingly become a socially and culturally diverse society. Immigrants and refugees from many different countries have made the United States their home of choice for a variety of reasons. Reasons to leave one's homeland and migrate vary from such things as opportunities for employment and economic advancement, higher education, religious freedom, and to avoid persecution due to political or social beliefs. In the more recent decades, many of the new ethnic groups that have come to the United States have chosen to retain their own cultural identity, including such things as language, religion, and cultural practices. According to the United States Census (2000), some forty-four million people living in America speak a language other than English in their own homes. Of these, close to twenty million people indicate that they speak very little or no English. Because of the trends to retain individual cultures, the United States of America has become increasingly a bilingual and bicultural society. The need for successful intercultural communication between helping professionals and migrants cannot be stressed enough.

According to Warner and Mochel (1998), culture is an integrated system of unconscious and learned behavior patterns that are characteristic of a group of people and that are not a result of biological inheritance. Warner and Mochel remind us that culture is learned and not something to which we are born. Further, culture is something that we share with members of society as a collective whole, and transmit this knowledge to children through parents and other significant adult role models.

Cultures set the guidelines for what is deemed as appropriate and inappropriate behaviors, ways of thinking and appropriate or inappropriate ways of expressing one's thoughts and emotions. Culture shapes the way people view the world around them. Further, culture shapes people's relationships with family, kin groups, neighbors, friends, community, and society as a whole. Culture is what shapes our institutions that make society a functional operating system, such as religious organizations, political entities, and economic systems. Above all else, culture is what shapes our beliefs, values, and ideals.

Many researchers who have examined immigration tend to view its impact in broad based societal terms. However, the issues that surround acculturation are usually found within the family unit. The family serves as the central social unit for most persons who migrate and the family dynamics demonstrate the interplay of individual, interpersonal, intrapersonal, and intergroup relationships. The manner in which immigrant or refugee families negotiate two opposing cultural systems, particularly when some members of the family acculturate more quickly than do other members, reveals a microcosm of both the conflicts and the processes by which adaptation defines the experience of migration (Hynie, 1997).

From a ecological perspective, adaptation refers to a person's capacity to adjust to his or her surrounding environment. Adaptation implies that a person must change or adjust to the new conditions or circumstances in order to continue effective functioning (Zastrow and Kirst-Asham, 1994).

Historically, the Hmong have learned to adapt to an ever changing surrounding environment and yet be able to maintain a unique sense of who they are as a people. Unlike many immigrants arriving in the United States of America today, the Hmong people were considered ethnic minorities within their own homelands and bring with them a unique sense of cultural distinctiveness (Quincy, 1997).

Cultural adaptation is affected by whether one member of an ethnic group migrated alone or with a larger group, such as his or her family, clan, or community. Families which migrate alone usually have a greater need to adapt quickly to the new host culture, as insignificant numbers of their group are available to establish a sense of community or common origin. When a number of families migrate together, as is the case with many of the Hmong families that came to the United States, the group is able to preserve much more of the traditions and customs, making adaptation and adjustment to the host culture more gradual and deliberate.

Awareness of the Hmong people in the United States has not necessarily meant an understanding of the culture. Often confused with Cambodians, Laotians, and Vietnamese, the Hmong people have migrated to the United States in large numbers over the past twenty years with little research available that examines the diversity and uniqueness of this group.

According to Sucheng Chan (1994), it is almost impossible to generalize how well the Hmong people have adapted to their new lives in the United States because their conditions in different regions of the country vary so greatly. The approximate 300,000 Hmong people residing in the United States span from the East to the West coastal regions with the largest populations presently residing in the states of Minnesota, Wisconsin and California (St. Olaf, 1997). In 1998 alone, some 20,000 Hmong people migrated to Minnesota from the state of California.

At the beginning of the new millennium, there was an estimated 42,000 Hmong refugees residing in various cities within the state of Minnesota with 34,000 Hmong people residing in the neighboring state of Wisconsin. The latest population figures indicate that forty-five percent of the Hmong people residing in the United States are now living in the midwestern states of Minnesota and Wisconsin (U.S. Census, 2000).

Since 1975, the United States of America has accepted over 110,000 refugees that have been identified as either Hmong or Laotian Highlanders. As a people, the Hmong trace their ancestry back to China over thousand of years ago.

To say the Hmong people have experienced cultural shock in their migration and resettlement to the United States would be an understatement. Many Hmong people still hold vivid memories of the East Asian Wars and harsh lives in Thai refugee camps. Yet, shortly after arrival to the United States, the Hmong people were expected to adapt to a highly industrialized and technologically driven society. The Hmong people have experienced barriers in language and communication, education, economics, employment, religion, cultural, and contrasting racial differences.

Many of the Hmong who arrived in the United States as refugees had never before lived in an urban setting. Many of the Hmong people had never before used electricity or been exposed to indoor plumbing within their homes in Asia. In addition, the Hmong people's traditional values of family, kin, and clan welfare was in direct and continuous conflict with the values of the American social welfare system as well as the American idealogies of independence and self-determination.

Resettlement to the United States of America has not necessarily been a solution to the problems faced by the Hmong people. The Hmong refugees have faced tremendous obstacles in the acculuturation process as they have attempted to adjust to a highly technological society from the more rural lives to which they had known. The accelerated lifestyle of the United States has resulted in turmoil, difficulties, and crises for a people who do not possess the necessary skills to successfully deal with the changes.

Highlights of the Methodology

Phenomenological Perspective

The research presented in this text addresses the question: *What affect does non-voluntary migration have on the acculturation levels as measured by cultural awareness and ethnic loyalty of the Hmong people residing in Rochester, Minnesota?* This study approaches the research question using a phenomenological perspective. The phenomenological perspective seeks to understand the life experiences of an individual and how that individual perceives the world around him. Phenomenological research is intended to answer the basic question: "What is it like to have a certain type of experience?" (Crabtree and Miller, 1992).

Qualitative research begins with a foreshadowed problem that is anticipated as a research question and then continuously reformulated during the data collection process. The continual reformulation of the research problem reflects the emergence of the research design. The reformulation of the research problem is anticipated and expected as data is collected and evaluated and as different research strategies acquire a total picture of the different subjects chosen for study. This results in what is called an "emerging research problem." (McMillian and Schumacher, 1997).

Limitations of the Research

The Hmong subjects who were selected for this study should not be considered as representative of all Hmong people who reside in the United States of America or even within the midwestern regions of the United States. The data that is presented here does not necessarily reflect all Hmong people and therefore cannot be generalized to other groups. The subject sample base was not randomly chosen and the subjects were asked if they would volunteer for the study, indicating a willingness of the subjects to participate.

A small group of Hmong persons living in Rochester, Minnesota was studied in-dept. Every effort was made to describe the subject sample demographically and whenever possible, compare the subjects used in this study to other Hmong people within the midwestern region of the United States.

Expectations for this Research

There is currently an estimated 42,000 Hmong refugees residing in Minnesota, which represents approximately twenty-three percent of the total Hmong refugee population residing in the United States. Over 20,000 Hmong refugees had migrated to the state of Minnesota from California in 1998 along (Lao Human Rights Council, 1998). This large migration of Hmong people to Minnesota from California in one short year is not a phenomenon that is easily explained.

Chao Thao (1998), believes that there is a direct parallel between secondary migration in the United States and the Hmong people's tradition of moving from one place to another in response to adverse and changing conditions. Thao also believes that the Hmong people may make these secondary moves within the United States to reunify with family members and clans, to improve family living conditions through higher welfare payments, to increase job opportunities, and to lower housing costs.

Sucheng Chan (1994), states that secondary migration of the Hmong people in the United States may also occur to increase the size of the Hmong population in a given community in order to maintain important social relationships that form the basis for Hmong people's ethnic identification.

The increase in the Hmong people's population in Rochester, Minnesota is the area of focus for this text. Without an adequate knowledge base of the needs of the Hmong refugees, psychologists, social workers, therapists, and other helping professionals may not be able to effectively aide the Hmong community in overcoming obstacles related to their accultruation and adaptation within this midwestern city.

The Hmong people are Rochester's newest migrants and there is to date no comprehensive or empirical information about this group of refugees and their acculturation process or basic needs as they adapt to the new host community.

Services that are available to the Hmong refugees of this region are quite sparse and fragmented. Few services in Rochester offer translation or specific programs that are targeted toward the Hmong people. As a group, the Hmong people have experienced high rates of unemployment with low levels of formal education and training that would be necessary in today's highly technological job market. The local Rochester area Hmong leaders have expressed their concern over high unemployment, low wages, and the lack of specific job skills of their clans. These problems are coupled with the loss of Federal dollars for refugees, which has created further complications and problems for the Rochester area Hmong.

To maximize productivity as new Americans and Minnesotans, the Hmong people will need provisions for equal opportunities in order to successfully adapt. Without an adequate understanding of the Rochester area Hmong people and their unique identity as well as unique needs, services and programs geared toward refugees will remain fragmented and ineffectual.

This study serves as a new knowledge base for understanding the Hmong people of the city of Rochester, Minnesota and their unique culture and current adaptation needs. This study was also designed to serve as a foundation in the formulation of workable strategies to respond to the needs of the Hmong refugees and to assist in empowering them to be active and involved members of the greater Rochester community.

REFERENCES

Chan, S., (1994). *Hmong Means Free: Life in Laos and America.* Philadelphia: PA: Temple University Press.

Crabtree, B., and Miller, W., (1992). *Doing Qualitative Research: Research Methods for Primary Care, Volume 3.* Newbury Park, CA: Sage Publications.

Encarta On-Line (1999). [online]. Available: http://encarta.msn.com/reference.

Encyclopedia Britannica (1999). [online]. Available: http://www.eb.com.

Haines, D., (1996). *Refugees in America in the 1990's.* Westport, CT: Greenwood Publishing Company.

Hein, J., (1997). The Hmong Cultural Repertoire: Explaining Cultural Variation Within an Ethnic Group. *Hmong Studies Journal.* 2.1. pp. 1-8.

Hynie, M., (1997). *From Conflict to Compromise. Immigrant Families and the Processes of Acculturation.* Montreal, CA: McGill University Press.

Koltyk, J., (1998). *New Pioneers in the Heartland: Hmong Life in Wisconsin.* Boston, MA: Allyn and Bacon Publishing.

Lao Human Rights Council, (1998). *About Lao Family Community of Minnesota.* [online]. Available: http://home.earthlink.net/~laohumrights/1998data.html.

McMillian J., and Schumacher, S., (1997). *Research in Education: A Conceptual Introduction (4th ed.).* New York, NY: Longman Press.

Quincy, K., (1997). *Hmong: History of a People.* Seattle, WA: University of Washington Press.

St. Olaf University (1997). *Hmong and Immigration: Frequently Asked Questions.* [online]. Available: http://www.stolaf.edu/people/cdr/hmong/faq/immigration.

Strand, P., and Woodrow, J., (1985). *Indochinese Refugees in America: Problems of Adaptation and Assimilation.* Durham, NC: Duke University Press.

Thao, C., (1988). *The Hmong in the West.* Minneapolis, MN: University of Minnesota.

U.S. Census Bureau (2000). *American Fact Finder Census.* [online]. Available: http://factfinder.census.gov/servlet.

Warner, M., and Mochel, M., (1998). The Hmong and Health Care in Merced, California. *Hmong Studies Journal.* 2.2. pp. 2-8.

Zastrow, C., and Kirst-Asham, K., (1994). *Understanding Human Behavior and the Social Environment (3rd ed.).* Chicago, IL: Nelson-Hall Publishers.

Chapter 2

The Melting Pot

In the early history of the Americas, European explorers conquered, claimed and reclaimed the land now referred to as the United States of America. The first immigrant colony established in the United States was in St. Augustine, Florida by the Spaniards in 1565 (Daniels, 1994). The number of people that arrived to the Americas following the initial settlement were coming to what was a vast, wild, open, and unsettled territory.

Laws and systems of governance were not formalized until 1776 and the formal incorporation of the United States of America. The first United States Census took place in the year 1790. In the late 18th century, sixty percent of the United States of America population were of British descent, with the majority of the remaining forty percent coming from English speaking areas of Europe. The United States Census of 1790 did not account for the African American slave population who were reportedly twenty percent of the total United States population at the time (Daniels, 1994)..

A century later, one of the largest immigration movements in the United States occurred. This massive wave of immigration occurred between the years 1840 to 1880 and brought people from Western and Northern European countries to a new land that was now known as the United States of America. There were no restrictions on migration at the time and many came to the United States of America fleeing political upheaval, war, famine, and poverty then occurring in their countries of origin (Fix and Passel, 1994).

The second major wave of immigration occurred in the early 1900's and consisted mainly of persons from Southern and Central Europe. This new wave of immigrants were in large part persons who did not speak English.

This resulted in the beginning debate and subsequent discussions on assimilation and acculturation within the United States of America.

Israel Zangwill in a poem written in 1909 was first to use the term melting pot. To Zangwill, the 'melting' of all ethnic cultures into something 'American' would be of the greatest benefit to the United States and society. Zangwill thus differed from those who derided the Un-American cultures, which were still being maintained in ethnic enclaves within major United States cities. Zangwill believed that ethnic cultures would make an important contribution to the eventual development of the 'Ultimate American Citizen', of which he assumed would reflect a 'blending' of all the representative cultures residing in the United States rather than from adoption of one particular Anglo culture (Park, 1950).

The 1920's brought new and more restrictive immigration laws to the United States. The Great Depression of the 1930's brought immigration to the United States at the lowest in recorded history. The first laws dealing with issues of immigration to the United States of America was the Immigration Act of 1891 and was passed in order to establish national control of immigration. This legislation created the Office for Immigration, which created categories for which people could be excluded from entering the United States. During this time in history, those who were excluded included criminals, polygamists, and people diagnosed with contagious diseases. This act set a precedent for exclusion which would eventually be expanded upon to include other 'less desirable' groups (Jensen, 1988).

The Immigration and Nationalization Act of 1924 was the first to set a numerical quota on immigration to the United States of America. The Immigration and Nationalization Act of 1924 created a ceiling of 150,000 Europeans per year that were able to immigrate to the United States. This act further barred Japanese from immigrating, and provided for admission of immigrants based on the proportion of national origin groups that were already represented in the United States according to the 1890 census records (Fix and Passel, 1994).

It was the Immigration and Nationality Act of 1965 which repealed quotas based on country of origin and replaced immigration laws with preference categories for immigration. The ultimate goal was to allow for family reunification based upon employment skills. Vast immigration that had never before been allowed to the United States suddenly became possible for many Asian immigrants, though many believed this act would bring more immigration from Southern European countries (Daniels, 1994).

The New Immigration Wave

By the 1990's, Asians had overtaken Hispanics as the largest growing minority population in the United States of America. The Asian population increased from 3.7 million in 1980 to 7.3 million a short decade later in 1990 (United States Bureau of Census, 1991). In recent years, immigrants from Asian countries has comprised close to half of all legal immigrants admitted to the United States, increasing from seven percent of all immigrants in 1965 to forty-six percent of all immigrants in 1990 (Edmonston and Passel, 1994).

In the 1990's, the number of immigrants making their way to Minnesota was about one third as many as in other states across the United States of America. A historical analysis released by the United States Census Bureau shows that 8.9 percent of all United States residents in 2000 were born elsewhere. That's up from 7.9 percent in 1990 and 4.7 percent in 1970 (U.S. Census, 2000). The peak period for foreign-born residents in the United States was at 14.9 percent in 1890.

Just as in the rest of the United States during the time, Minnesota's peak migration period was in the 1890's when immigrants from Sweden, Germany, and Ireland moved to the state in record numbers. Senior Census Bureau Demographer, Campbell Gibson, states that the number of foreign-born people in the United States climbed by six million from 1990 to 1997.

Hispanics and Asians were the greatest source of new immigrant population increased in the state. According to Gibson, the Midwest has not been a major recipient of immigrants in the last generation. Hyman Berman, a University of Minnesota historian reported that even though Minnesota had only seen a six- percent increase in immigrants during the past decade, this was a significant change from prior decades, because the groups arriving were different from what was seen in the past. In 1990, 12,000 Asians migrated to Minnesota, over half of the 23,000 foreign born immigrants in Minnesota for that year (Rochester Post Bulletin, 1999).

According to the Winona Daily News (2001), the migration of Hmong from California to Minnesota and Wisconsin during the past decade has established the Midwest as the "Heart of the Hmong Community" in the United States of America.

Theories of Assimilation

Since the beginning of the 20th century, researchers have used the concept of assimilation to describe the process of minority groups adaptation to the majority group's values, norms, and belief systems (Park, 1950).

As a theoretical framework for studying immigrants arriving in the United States of America, the assimilation perspective views immigrant adaptation to the host culture as a linear process whereby the immigrant gives up cultural values, norms, and behaviors from the country of origin and replaces these with the cultural values, beliefs, and norms of the host country.

Robert Park's formulation of the assimilation theory was one of the earliest known and most influential for its time. Park's 'Race Relations Cycle,' held the basic premise that plant and animal ecology can be applicable to human social order. Competition and conflict between groups appear as natural, as does the resulting accommodation of each group to the needs and demands of the other. The ultimate state in Park's Race Relations Cycle was that assimilation of one group naturally occurs to the other. Park considered this as a 'melting pot approach to assimilation' (Park, 1950).

Cultural Diversity in the United States of America

The United States of America experienced the greatest rise in immigration in the last 100 years. More than one million legal and undocumented immigrants and refugees arrive in the United States on an annual basis. The majority of immigrants and refuges come from Asian and Hispanic countries. Asian-born Americans now outnumber the European-born ones in the United States.

In Los Angeles, four in ten residents are foreign-born and in New York City, three in ten are foreign-born. By the end of the 20th century, white Americans were becoming an increasing minority. Ethnic identity has always been a central component of life in the United States of America. The salience of ethnicity is probably related to the fact that white ethnic groups are slowing becoming the minority populations of the United States (McGoldrick, Giordano, and Pearce, 1996).

Immigrant and refugee family members vary in how much of their heritage is retained and at the rate in which they will acquire English and Anglo-cultural skills. The language of the culture of origin is a principle factor in preserving one's own culture. The east and west coasts are frequently the point of entry for many immigrants and refugees. As a result, the coastal cities are the most likely to have ethnically diverse neighborhoods.

Ethnically diverse neighborhoods can serve as a temporary refuge against the stressors of migration that usually surface within the family's second generation. Those immigrant and refugee families who make their way to areas where the population is relatively homogenous and stable, such as in the Midwestern United States, generally have more problems with adjustment and are forced to adapt more rapidly (McGoldrick, Giordano, and Pearce, 1996).

The struggle for ethnic survival has been true of many groups that are distinguishable on the basis of culture of origin, race, and religion. The experience of practically all new ethnic groups in the United States has been on of initial turmoil and hardship as they attempt to fit into their new host culture.

The United States of America has increasingly become a more culturally diverse and ethnically rich place to live. Immigrants and refugees from many countries have made the United States their homeland for various reasons such as seeking economic advancement or higher education, freedom to practice one's religion, and escape from political strive and persecution. In the more recent decades, many of these new ethnically diverse groups have made a conscious choice to retain their cultural identity, including language, cultural and religious practices. These factors have led to a raise in a more bilingual and bicultural American society, which has increased the need for adaptive and successful intercultural communication.

Many ethnic groups who live in the United States of America's pluralistic society experience sociocultural dissonance or the undue stress and incongruence caused by belonging to two distinctly different cultures – the ethnic culture of origin and the dominant culture of the host society.

Chau (1989) suggests that ethnic groups live within the context of a sustaining environment where institutional structures of the dominant society provide the services necessary for survival in the host culture. At the same time, ethnically diverse persons attempt to draw upon the resources of their own culture and seek the nurturing environment from their own ethnic group. This nurturing environment is the immediate ethnic community that shapes individual psychological, sociological, and cultural identity from childhood and continues to provide affective nurturing support well into old age.

For many ethnic minority groups, sociocultural dissonance is quite stressful. Differences in status and culture, prejudice directed toward them directly or indirectly, unfamiliarity with the host environment, and restricted access to necessary services for survival can exacerbate the stress and conflict felt by many ethnic minority persons.

Stress, disorientation, and other personal reactions can be considered a normal response to a transcultural move or to the uprooting of one's customary resource and support network (Chau, 1989).

The changing ethnic demographics in the United States of America have had a significant impact on all aspects of the American society. Examining the workforce of the new millennium, eighty percent are now women, ethnic minorities, or new immigrants and refugees. This reality in the context of a growing global economy helps to explain the interest in many management firms to examine cultural diversity within organizations and work environments.

More than five million children of immigrant and refugee parents are now enrolled in the public schools of the United States since the 1990's, with approximately three and a half million who come from homes where English is not the first language spoken. More than 150 different languages are currently represented in the American public school system (Thomas, 1991).

The fluidity of cultural identity has been an American tradition. However, a conservative backlash against multiculturalism has been developing as noted by the resurgence of white extremist skinheads and Neo-Nazi groups that foster hatred and anti-immigrant nativism. According to these extremist groups, multiculturalism is criticized as a corruption in our educational system and ultimately destroys our country's national cohesion (Schleshinger, 1995).

Understanding Ethnic Identification

Ethnic identification is important to individuals at a number of different levels. Other members of society may see a group as ethnically different even if they may express very little interest in ethnicity or cultural diversity. Ethnic identification can be based on visible traits of a minority person such as physical characteristics, manner or expression, or dress or not so obvious traits such as one's surname or family customs (Gelfand, 1993).

By definition, all ethnic groups have a distinct and unique culture. According to DeVos and Romanci-Ross (1995), *"an ethnic group is a self-perceived group of people who hold in common a set of traditions not shared by others."*

Hein (1997) defined ethnicity as: *"Shared beliefs, norms, values, preference, in-group memories, loyalties, and consciousness in kind."*

Hein goes on to elaborate, *"An ethnic group is a segment of a larger society whose members have thought, by themselves and others, to have a common origin and to share important segments of a common culture and who, in addition, participate in shared activities in which the common origin and culture are significant ingredients. "*

Ethnicity, according to McGoldrick, Giordano, and Pearce (1996), refers to one's common ancestry through which customs are shared and values have evolved over a period of time. Ethnicity is deeply tied into the family of origin from which values and customs are transmitted to future generations by the family and are reinforced by the surrounding community.

Ethnicity has a powerful influence in determining one's own basic sense of identity. A sense of belonging and history is basic to individual psychological and sociological needs. A person may chose to ignore ethnicity or deny it by changing their name or rejecting family beliefs, social backgrounds, and cultural customs, but to do is to the detriment of one's own sense of personal well being.

According to Greely (1969), the subject of personal ethnicity can evoke deep feelings and discussions of ethnic backgrounds can become polarized or judgmental depending upon the perception of ethnicity by the persons discussing it. Using presumed common cultural origin to define who 'we' are and who 'they' are seems to touch on the most basic and primordial parts of the human psyche.

The concept of an ethnic group's sense of peoplehood is based on a combination of race, religion, and cultural history. This sense of peoplehood is retained, whether or not members realize their commonalties with one and other. The consciousness or unconsciousness of ethnic identity varies greatly within groups and from one cultural group to another.

Ethnicity interplay's with economics, race, class, religion, politics, geography, and the length of time since a group migrated from one place to another. The group's particular historical perspective and collective experiences, and the degree of discrimination experienced all play key roles in one's sense of peoplehood (McGoldrick, Giordano, and Pearce, 1996, Greely, 1969). The impact of war, terrorism, and political upheaval and oppression, such as the experiences of the Hmong in the 1970's can have a direct affect on the view of the ethnic group's historical customs and traditions.

According to Warner and Mochel (1998), culture is an integrated system of unconscious and conscious learned behavioral patterns that are characterized by an ethnic group and are not the result of biological traits or inheritance. Warner and Mochel point out that culture is a learned trait and is shared by members of the group in a collective whole, and transmitted to children by the parents and significant and influential adult role models.

Culture sets the guidelines for appropriate behaviors, styles of thinking, and appropriate ways of expressing one's emotions. Culture shapes the way a person views the outside world. Culture shapes relationships with family, kin groups, neighbors, and friends. It shapes economic, political, and religious institutions. Above all, culture shapes one's beliefs, values, and ideals.

REFERENCES

Chau, K., (1989). Sociocultural Dissonance Among Ethnic Minority Populations. *Social Casework* 70. pp 224-239.

Daniels, R., (1974). *Coming to America: A History of Immigration and Ethnicity In American Life.* New York City, NY: Harper Collins.

DeVos, G., and Romanci-Ross, L., (1995). *Ethnic Identity: Creation, Conflict, and Accommodation.* Walnut Creek, CA: Altamira Press.

Edmonston, B., and Passel, J.S., (1994). *Immigration and Ethnicity: The Integration of America's Newest Arrivals.* Washington, DC: The Urban Institute Press.

Fix, M., and Passel, J., (1994). *Immigration and Immigrants: Setting the Record Straight.* Washington, DC: The Urban Institute Press.

Gelfand, D., (1993). *Aging and Ethnicity: Knowledge and Services.* New York City, NY: Springer Publishing Company.

Greely, A., (1969). *Why Can't They Be Like Us?* New York City, NY: American Jewish Community Press.

Hein, J., (1997). The Hmong Cultural Repertoire: Explaining Cultural Variation Within an Ethnic Group. *Hmong Studies Journal.* 2.1. pp. 1-8.

Hmong Moving Eastward: Census Data Show Heart of Hmong Community Moves to Upper Midwest. (2001, August 16). The Winona Daily News. A1.

Immigration to Midwest has Slowed: New Arrivals More Visible than Before. (1999, March 9). The Rochester Post Bulletin. A.1.

Jensen, J., (1988). *Passage from India: Asian Indians in North America.* New Haven, CT: Yale University Press.

McGoldrick, M., Giordano, J., and Pearce, J., (1996). *Ethnicity and Family Therapy (2nd Ed.).* New York City, NY: Guilford Press.

Park, R., (1950). *Race and Culture.* Glencoe, IL: Free Press.

Schleshinger, A., (1995). *The Disuniting of America: Reflections on a Multicultural Society.* New York City, NY: Norton Press.

Thomas, R., (1991). *Beyond Race and Gender.* New York City, NY: American Management Association.

U.S. Census Bureau (1991). *USGS Geographic Names Information System.* [online]. Available: http://www.census.gov/cgi-bin/gazetteer.

U.S. Census Bureau (2000). *American Fact Finder Census.* [online]. Available: http://factfinder.census.gov/servlet.
Warner, M., and Mochel, M., (1998). The Hmong and Health Care in Merced, California. *Hmong Studies Journal.* 2.2 pp.2-8..

Chapter 3

The Process of Acculturation

Acculturation is the process that occurs when an individual from one culture comes into contact with another culture. Models for studying acculturation have changed over this past century. More recent and current models consider multidimensional aspects of acculturation and view cultural identification with separate and unique ethnic groups as possible and ideal (Edmonston and Passel, 1994).

Gil, Vega, and Dimas (1994), differentiated between acculturation or cultural change and acculturation stress or the stress that results from the process of cultural change. Some stress may be endemic to this process, the result of communication problems, differences in cultural values, and the experiences resulting from long term and constant discrimination. However, some ethnic minority families appear able to move through the acculturation process experiencing less stress than other families do.

One factor that has been implicated as a contributing factor to acculturation stress is the development of different levels of acculturation that occurs between immigrant and refugee parents and their children. These acculturation gaps are caused by the children's increased identification with the American culture and with their decreased identification with their family of origin's culture. In turn, this acculturation gap may exacerbate existing family difficulties, which result in communication problems and child to parent conflicts (Szapocznik, Rio, Perez-Vidal, Kurtines, Hervis, and Santisteban (1986).

Through the process of acculturation, refugee and immigrant families incorporate themselves into a dominant culture by adopting the dominant cultural attitudes, norms, and values.

Immigrant and refugee families externally will adopt normative behaviors and social patterns found acceptable to the dominant group, but they can also retain behavioral patterns unique to their own cultural group (Marden, Meyer, and Engel, 1992).

Within the acculturation process, immigrants and refugees may forsake their own cultural heritage in order to fit in with the dominant culture. Assimilation is the process that occurs when a minority group integrates itself into the dominant group's culture. Eventually, the minority group fuses with the majority group, so that the two become virtually indistinguishable by their own cultural characteristics.

Schaefer (1996), believes that in order to become a complete process, assimilation must entail a conscious and active effort by the minority group member. This involves ridding oneself of all distinguishing characteristics and beliefs, and also the complete acceptance of the minority group member by the dominant society.

In turn, accommodation is the result of a stable coexistence between the majority and minority groups. Each group takes the other for granted and both the groups accept the same rationalizations for the existing majority and minority cultural patterns. This mutual accommodation of majority and minority groups is the result of the acculturation process that occurs for minority members into the dominant culture. A possible end result of this process is total assimilation into the majority society.

Immigrants and refugees often experience marginality when they strive to be accepted by the dominant society. They may attempt to emulate the dominant group, but continue to remain peripheral to it. Although the minority group may share the normative goals of the dominant group, the members of the minority group remain outside and attempt to coexist between the two differing cultures. Conflicts of values, expectations, and loyalties characterize some of the struggles experienced by marginality (Schaefer, 1996).

The adjustment process experienced by Asian immigrants and refugees in the United States of America has been influenced by their status as non-whites. Immigrants and refugees are faced with many obstacles that often delay their economic and social integration into the American society. Prejudice and discrimination against foreign-born people, lack of adequate English speaking skills, and unfamiliarity with the American customs, education, and job market are just a few of the many difficulties faced by new immigrants and refugees to the United States.

The process of integration into the dominant society often takes several generations within the immigrant or refugee family, and varies across families and dimensions (Edmonston and Passel, 1994). For example, acculturation or the learning of such things as English language, manner of American dress, and the like is generally quickly and easily achieved by the second generation. Structural and broader social integration into American society generally takes much longer because immigrant and refugee families often struggle with being completely accepted by the majority group members and the longer, more settled, and established groups.

Researchers of immigrant and refugee groups have a tendency to examine the issue of acculturation in broad based societal terms. However, the issues surrounding acculturation are usually acted out within the family unit. Not only is the family the central social unit for most immigrants and refugees, family dynamics demonstrate the interplay of individual, interpersonal, and intergroup relationships.

The manner in which immigrant and refugee families negotiate the two opposing cultural systems, especially when some family members acculturate more quickly than other members, reveals a microcosm of both the conflicts and the processes of adaptation that define the experience of the immigrant or refugee (Hynie, 1997).

Padilla and Keefe (1987), presented a model of acculturation that involved the elements of cultural awareness and ethnic loyalties. Cultural awareness refers to the individual's prior knowledge of specific cultural material of the host culture as compared to one's own culture. This would include things such as language, values, history, foods, etc. Ethnic loyalty refers to the immigrant or refugee member's individual preferences of one cultural orientation over another.

For many immigrant and refugee groups, identity, comfort, and safety are within the boundaries of one's own cultural group. To be outside the in-group means they must leave that comfort zone and attempt to adapt to a new out-group setting.

Dashefsky (1976), attempted to provide a conceptualization of identity that can be applied to ethnicity. An individual's identity can be defined by the individual or by others. However, alternative criteria form the basis for these definitions. When an individual's identity is defined by other people it is known as social identity. Social identity may be based on a number of broad categorical attributes, including one's occupation, ethnicity, and age. Personal identity is based not on these broader attributes, but rather on elements that are unique to a specific individual. Personal identity attributes include such things as family relationships, external relationships, and general personality traits.

Personal stories, views of reality, and adaptive behaviors are anchored in the life experiences of an individual's race, ethnicity, and social status.

The most fundamental dislocation of migration is the uprooting of a structure of cultural meanings, which can be likened to the roots that sustain and nourish a plant. With the disruption of lifelong attachments, internal and external meanings of reality are severely challenged. New reality contexts of life and society are slowly generated by the immigrant or refugee in order to experience new meaning and ultimately adaptation into the mainstream (Marris, 1980).

The uprooting of established norms and values as well as exposure to a new culture can create various types of psychological distress, including cultural shock, marginality, social alienation, psychological conflict, psychosomatic symptoms and post-traumatic stress for new immigrants and refugees (Zamichow, 1992).

Over a period of time, many symptoms related to acculturation will decrease as the immigrant or refugee gains language skills and cultural competence. Acculturation theory assumes that maintaining, rather than shedding of one's culture of origin and language increased the mental and physical risks of immigrants.

Portes and Rambaut (1990), challenged the views that assimilation is desirable and necessary for successful adjustment. Portes and Rambaut attest that assimilation is not the solution to immigrant stress and report that immigrants and refugees who attempt to become more Americanized may have more psychological problems than those who retain their language, cultural ties, rituals and traditions.

A more recent view on acculturation come from LaFramboise, Coleman, and Gerton, (1993). Alteration Theory assumes that it is possible to know two distinct cultures and languages, and to appropriately use this information in differing contexts and environments without giving up one for the other. Rouse (1992), coined the term "cultural bifocality" to define the individual capacity of an immigrant or refugee to see the world through two very distinct value lens.

A suggested model of culture (Miyares, 1998), presents the following components: 1. Ethnolinguistic; 2. Ideological; 3. Sociopolitical and; 4. Economic. The artifacts and art of a culture are physical manifestations of these components. The ethnolinguistic component is the most enduring for ethnic groups. This refers to one's ethnic self-identification, a perception that can continue for many generations after the immigrant or refugee groups initial emigration. Spoken language may change, as well as one's citizenship status, yet a person's emotional affiliations to his or her country and culture of origin may remain.

The second component of this cultural model is ideological. This refers to one's world view and belief systems. The third component of culture is sociopolitical. This component often results in the greatest internal conflicts due to the migration experience itself. Political and social practices may change as the civic culture of the new community is learned. Traditional political and social culture may continue on a limited or a redefined basis. The culture's political climate refers to perceptions of power, leadership, and social position, as well as the relationships between individuals and the group.

The fourth component of culture is economic. This component is strongly influenced by the sociopolitical and ideological components in defining values and acceptable methods of social and economic exchange.

Ethnic Identity

Ethnic minorities often try to maintain their ethnic identification while seeking inclusion in the dominant culture's mainstream. Among the factors that form ethnic identity are one's skin color, name, language, common religious beliefs, ancestry, heritage, and place of origin (Lum, 1996). As Lum suggests, "ethnicity is a powerful unifying force that gives the individual a sense of belonging based on commanality."

The United States of America consists of a multitude of persons representing various racial and ethnic groups. These persons differ among many dimensions including cultural history, socioeconomic status, geographic locations, and intergenerational relationships. The terms minority and majority groups are used to designate group differences among power, class, and prestige dimensions (Dilworth, Burton, and Johnson, 1993).

The dimensions of power, class, and prestige are differentiated by the group members rights to economic, social, and political power systems (Taylor, 1994). Persons who belong to ethnic minority groups are purported to have less influence within social, political, and economic systems when compared to persons within the majority group (Dilworth, Burton, and Johnson, 1993). In the United States of America, it is the white majority group that defines features of society such as language, ideology, religion, and definitions of beauty (Perry and Perry, 1993).

The extent to which persons spend time with members of their own ethnic group influences the life course they will adopt (Barresi, 1987). Ethnic communities are a source of social and emotional support and help to preserve a sense of self identity. Participation in an ethnic social network influences the maintenance of one's ties to culture (Ujimoto, 1987).

An individual's self conception is formed by the attributes held by that individual based on ethnic group membership, gender, age, religious affiliation, education, and occupation. On the other hand, deep-rooted, less conscious ideals of the individual's ego identity may not be so apparent unless they are brought to surface through intensive probing. It is highly probable that these unconscious ideals are a crucial component of ethnic identification.

Ethnic identification may be important at a number of differing levels for an individual. The individual may be seen as ethnically different by other members of society even though he or she expresses very little interest in the ethnic culture of origin.

This ethnic identification may be based on visible traits such as physical characteristics and manner in which one dresses. As acculturation levels increase for an individual, ease of ethnic identification based on visible traits becomes more difficult and others may need to rely increasingly on more unpredictable indicators such as one's surname (Dashefsky, 1976).

Adaptation to the Host Society

Adaptation, from an ecological perspective, refers to an individual's capacity to adapt to the surrounding environmental conditions. Adaptation implies that a person must change or adjust to the new conditions and circumstances in the environment in order to continue effectively functioning (Zastrow and Kirst-Asham, 1994).

Of all immigrants to the United States, the refugee family feels the tension of adaptation most keenly. Acculturation is part of the consequences of the wrenching transition when refugees leave their country of origin and start a new life that was not voluntarily chosen.

Refugee families can experience a great deal of turmoil and tension in the process of adaptation and transition to the new culture. Often, the older family members will hold onto their language and cultural traditions indefinitely, while their younger family members will embrace the host society, thus adapting to American ways. Clashes between the generations within a refugee family is almost an inevitable certainty (Taylor-Hayes, 1999).

Milton Gordon's Model for Assimilation

Milton Gordon (1964), developed a working scale of assimilation for ethnic groups. In Gordon's model of assimilation, ethnic groups may move through a number of steps, although they will not necessarily pass through each stage. Some ethnic groups may skip stages of assimilation entirely.

Gordon composed the concept of assimilation into seven different dimensions: 1. Cultural assimilation or acculturation; 2. Structural assimilation or entrance into the social groups and institutions of the majority or host society on a large scale; 3. Marital assimilation or large-scale intermarriage with majority group members; 4. Identificational assimilation or a sense of identity that comes solely from the host society; 5. Attitude receptional assimilation or the absence of prejudice about the host society members; 6. Behavior receptional assimilation or the absence of discrimination against the host society members; 7. Civic assimilation or absence of value and power conflict with the host society.

In the final assimilation stage, the ethnic group abandons any identification with their ethnic background of origin. Instead of maintaining an ethnically based culture, the group accepts what Gordon termed, "Anglo-Conformity". Anglo-Conformity assumes the desirability of maintaining English institutions such as, the English language and English oriented cultural patterns as dominant and a standard for American life.

The first stage of Anglo-Conformity is behavioral assimilation or "acculuturation". The process of behavioral assimilation is one whereby the immigrant group adapts to the host society. This adaptation enables the ethnic group to survive physically and economically in the new host environrment.

Gordon argued that structural assimilation was the most crucial step in acculturation, because when this occurs, all other types of assimilation would eventually follow. Structural assimilation occurs after the ethnic group members have successfully achieved acculturation into the mainstream society.

White majority members who have resisted structural assimilation recognize its importance and fear racially based intermingling or miscegenation. Their resistance to integration indicates an understanding of the effects of the primary association between racial and ethnic groups (Gordon, 1982).

With successful acculturation, it may be possible for minority ethnic group members to intermingle with persons from other ethnic backgrounds, including those whose social status may be considered more desirable. Intermingling in voluntary organizations, clubs, and cliques only increases the chances that the next stage of intermarriage or amalgamation will occur.

Ethnic groups that are allowed to enter primary cliques and intermarry within the dominant society are more likely to develop a sense of identity with the dominant or majority group. This could result in a total abandonment of the minority ethnic groups prior cultural identification. This stage of assimilation is denoted by Gordon as identificational. Ethnic groups that come to be valued and accepted by the dominant society will reach a point where they experience little prejudice or discrimination.

As a result, the minority ethnic group may actually alter their beliefs to eliminate issues of value, priveledge, and power that previously differentiated them from the majority group. These latter stages of assimilation are called attitudinal receptional, behavioral receptional, and civic assimilation. Civic assimilation may not occur even though an minority ethnic group has progressed through all the other stages and has abandoned any individual sense of peoplehood.

Gordon's assimilation perspective makes several assumptions that many cultural researchers have criticized. This assimilation model often views immigration adaptation as an all or nothing proposition. Gordon's model assumes that values, norms, and behaviors of the immigrant or refugee's culture of origin are so incompatible with the American values, norms, and behaviors that the immigrant must eventually replace one with the other. This model also assumes that there is a need for immigrants and refugees to adapt, without addressing the diversity of very distinctly different social groups that exist within the host culture.

Gordon's assimilation model does not deal with the social stratification by race and ethnicity so evident in life within the United States of America that has a major impact on immigrants and refugees when they arrive here. By emphasizing the incorporation of immigrants into the mainstream dominant culture, Gordon's assimilation model ignores the role of ethnic social groups within the adaptation process for new immigrants and refugees. Further, Gordon's model does not allow for the possibility of reverse assimilation (Portes and Stepick, 1994), in which the majority group may also change as a result of contact and interaction with the minority group.

In spite of Gordon's assimilation model's flaws, the basic assumptions of the assimilation process, its emphasis on the power of exposure to aspects of the dominant host culture, such as the English language and the importance of participation in community life, are useful ideas that have been used and expanded upon in other theories of adaptation.

Glazer (1993), has questioned the viability of the concept of assimilation in the United States of America. Glazer argues that the ideology of assimilation has been challenged primarily because of the lack of incorporation of African-Americans into the dominant culture. Glazer attributes this to the discriminatory and prejudicial attitudes and behaviors exhibited toward African-Americans by the majority culture.

Those ethnic groups that have integrated into the political, educational, and economic institutions of the dominant society may be said to have assimilated themselves structurally. Simultaneously, however, these same ethnic groups may still maintain their ethnic identity through primary relationships in their private lives. Ethnicity is primarily an issue of identity and it will endure as long as it facilitates self-expression or it can be used in the competition for scarce resources.

Although Glazer's work does provide an arguable point regarding assimilation, what is not mentioned in his work are the varied degrees of exposure to the majority or dominant society by differing members of an extended ethnic minority family. Many ethnic minorities do not make a conscious decision about whether to utilize their ethnic background as a basis for self identification. Many first generation immigrants and refugees in the past have attempted to acculturate more quickly in order to survive in the dominant society while still holding on to the cultural roots which provided a sense of comfort in coping with the new or host environment.

Second generation Americans were historically able to gain more knowledge in the business and bureaucratic worlds as well as gain competency in the English language. Their ethnic heritage was not necessarily a refuge, but rather an embarrassing reminder of a period when their parents slaved in sweatshops in order to survive while being preyed upon by a wide variety of merchants, employers, and politicians.

Many second generation individuals would move away from their family's ethnic community. Some even would change their surnames to more Anglo-Saxon sounding ones, an often culminating step in the process of assimilation. The return to one's ethnic identity was often more a choice for third generation family members. Having economic, social, and psychological security, these grandchildren of the original immigrants and refugees could decide for themselves whether to ignore or embrace some of the more interesting and less restrictive components of their ethnic culture or origin (Gelfand, 1993).

Cultural Pluralism

Cultural pluralism argues that the differences between ethnic groups tend to persist despite substantial assimilation to differing levels. Trela and Sokolovsky (1979), distinguished between integrated and invidious pluralism. Integrated pluralism refers to the coexistence of distinct yet in many ways, similar ethnic groups without patterns of subordination of some groups by others. Invidious pluralism refers to a situation in which ethnic status is the basis of subordination of some groups by other groups. This model of cultural pluralism emphasizes ethnic differences that persist even from within the culture of origin.

Segmented Assimilation Theory

Portes and Zhou (1995), introduced the concept of segmented assimilation to describe three possible processes to adaptation for children of immigrants and refugees. Portes and Zhou argued that immigration since 1965 has been different from previous immigration to the United States of America and that studies have focused on the immigrants and refugees themselves which does not give insight into the adaptation process for the next generation. In their framework, there are three possible paths to segmented assimilation: 1. Adaptation and integration into the white middle classes; 2. Adaptation to the underclasses and a condition of permanent and sustained poverty; 3. Socioeconomic adaptation that occurs along with maintenance of strong cultural ties within an ethnic community.

Portes and Zhou's framework allows for the possibility that immigrant and refugee adaptation is not an all or nothing venture, but rather a minority ethnic culture can become part of the dominant host culture, yet continue to hold onto the ethnic institutions of the immigrant or refugee culture of origin. The end result is a direct benefit to the first and second generation immigrant and refugee groups. This framework takes into account the affect of stratification by race and ethnicity and its impact on immigrant and refugee families. This framework also supports the notion that some cases of second generation immigrant and refugee families who participate actively in their own ethnic communities do better in school than those who are more distant from their ethnic community (Zhou and Bankston, 1999).

Massey and Denton (1994), share that many features of post-1965 immigration distinguishes itself from previous waves of immigration and that these changes lead to a slower and possibly very different type of adaptation process. Massey and Denton hypothesize that the most recent wave of immigrants and refugees will be sustained within their own cultural identities for a longer period of time, as opposed to European immigrants at the turn of the century.

New immigrants and refugees are entering a highly stratified economy in the United States of America that is characterized by a dual labor market, in which movements from the secondary sector to the primary sector jobs require a higher educational level and more specialized technical skills. This specialized market place may be out of reach for many first and second generation immigrants and refugees. Finally, the geographic destinations of new immigrants and refugees within the United States have historically been highly concentrated in coastal and urban areas. Massey and Denton predict that the increasing levels of ethnic and racial concentrations within certain areas of the United States will lead to the existence of large foreign language and ethnic communities that will sustain themselves across several generations.

In summation, segmented assimilation theory takes into account the unique aspects of recent immigrant and refugee patterns and predicts that there are three different adaptation patterns that children of immigrants and refugees can follow. A key variable in this adaptation process is the social context of the ethnic group and the children who live in concentrated ethnic communities, thus taking advantage of the ethnic community's social capital (Portes, 1996).

Segmented assimilation theory hypothesizes that the minority ethnic community exerts a powerful influence on children of immigrants and refugees and that the children who participate within their own culture of origin may be as successful, if not more so, than those who identify with the dominant or mainstream society.

REFERENCES

Barresi, C.M., (1987). Ethnic Aging and the Life Course. In D.E. Gelfand and C.M. Barresi (Eds.). *Ethnic Dimensions of Aging*. New York City, NY: Springer Publishing Company.

Dashefsky, A., (1976). *Ethnic Identity in Society*. Chicago, IL: Rand-McNally.

Dilworth-Anderson, P., Burton, L., and Johnson, L., (1993). Reframing Theories for Understanding Race, Ethnicity and Families. In P.G. Boss, W. Doherty, R. LaRossa, W.R. Schumm, and S.K. Steinmetz (Eds.). *Handbook for Family Theories and Methods: A Contextual Approach*. New York City, NY: Plenum Press.

Edmonston, B., and Passel, J.S., (1994). *Immigration and Ethnicity: The Integration of America's Newest Arrivals*. Washington, DC: The Urban Institute Press.

Gelfand, D., (1993). *Aging and Ethnicity: Knowledge and Services*. New York City, NY: Springer Publishing Company.

Gil, A.G., Vega, W.A., and Dimas, J., (1994). Acculturation Stress and Personal Adjustment Among Hispanic Adolescent Boys. *Journal of Community Psychology*. 22. Pp. 43-54.

Glazer, N., (1993). Public Education and American Pluralism. In J. Coleman (Ed.). *Parents, Teachers, and Children: Prospects for Choice in American Education*. San Francisco, CA: Institute for Contemporary Studies Press.

Gordon, M., (1964). Assimilation in America: Theory and Reality. *Daedalus*, 90.2. pp. 263-285.

Gordon, M., (1982). *Assimilation in American Life*. New York City, NY: Oxford University Press.

Hynie, M., (1997). *From Conflict to Compromise: Immigrant Families and the Processes of Acculturation*. Montreal, Canada: McGill Uinversity Press.

LaFramboise, T., Coleman, H., and Gerton, J., (1993). Psychological Impact of Biculturalism: Evidence and Theory. *Psychological Bulletin*. 114.3. pp. 395-412.

Lum, D., (1996). *Social Work Practice and People of Color: A Process-Stage Approach*. Pacific Grove, CA: Brooks/Cole Publishing Company.

Marden, C., Meyer, G., and Engel, M., (1992). *Minorities in American Society (6th ed.)*. New York City, NY: Harper Collins Publishing.

Marris, P., (1980). The Uprooting of Meaning. In G.V. Goelho and P. Ahmed (Eds.). *Uprooting and Development: Dilemmas of Coping with Modernization*. New York City, NY: Plenum Press.

Massey, D., and Denton, N., (1994). *American Apartheid: Segregation and the Making of the Underclass*. Cambridge, MA: Harvard University Press.

Miyares, I.M., (1998). *The Hmong Refugee Experience in the United States*. New York City, NY: Garland Publishing, Inc.

Padilla, A.M., and Keefe, S.E., (1987). *Chicano Ethnicity (1st ed.)*. Albuquerque, NM: University of New Mexico Press.

Perry, J., and Perry, E., (1993). *The Social Web (6th ed.)*. New York City, NY: Harper Collins.

Portes, A., (1996). *The New Second Generation*. New York City, NY: Russell Sage Foundation.

Portes, A., and Rambaut, R., (1990). *Immigrant America: A Portrait*. Berkeley, CA: University of California Press.

Portes, A., and Stepick, A., (1994). *City on the Edge: The Transformation of Miami*. Berkeley, CA: University of California Press.

Portes, A., and Zhou, M., (1995). *Chinatown: The Socioeconomic Potential of an Urban Enclave: Conflicts in Urban and Regional Development*. Philadelphia, PA: Temple University Press.

Rouse, R., (1992). Making Sense of Settlement: Class Transformation, Cultural Struggle, and Transnationalism Among Mexican Immigrants in the United States. In N.G. Shiller, L. Basch, and C. Blanc-Szanton (Eds.). *Towards a Transnational Perspective on Migration: Race, Class, Ethnicity, and Nationalism Reconsidered*. New York City, NY: Academy of Sciences.

Schaefer, R.T., (1996). *Racial and Ethnic Groups (6th ed.)*. New York City, NY: Harper Collins Publishing.

Szapocznik, J., Rio, A., Perez-Vidal, A., Kurtines, W., Hervis, O., and Santisteban, D., (1986). Bicultural Effectiveness Training (BET): An Experimental Test of an Intervention Modality for Families Experiencing Integenerational/ Intercultural Conflict. *Hispanic Journal of Behavioral Sciences.* 8. pp. 303-331.

Taylor, R.L., (1994). *Ethnic Families in the United States: A Multicultural Perspective.* Englewood Cliffs, NJ: Prentice Hall.

Taylor-Hayes, K., *Tested by the Past: Torn by the Future.* (1999, February 26). The Minneapolis Star Tribune. A4-A8.

Trela, J.E., and Sokolovsky, J.H., (1979). Culture, Ethnicity and Policy for the Aged. In D.E. Gelfand and A.J. Kutzik (Eds.). *Ethnicity and Aging: Theory, Research, and Policy.* New York City, NY: Springer Publishing Company.

Ujimoto, K., (1987). Organizational Activities, Cultural Factors and Well-Being Of Aged Japanese Canadians. In D.E. Gelfand and C.M. Barresi (Eds.). *Ethnic Dimensions of Aging.* New York City, NY: Spring Publishing Company.

Zamichow, N., *No Way to Escape Fear.* (1992, February 10). The Los Angeles Times. B1-B3.

Zastrow, C., and Kirst-Asham, K., (1994). *Understanding Human Behavior and The Social Environment (3rd ed.)*. Chicago, IL: Nelson-Hall Publishing.

Zhou, M., and Bankston, C., (1999). *Growing Up American: How Vietnamese Children Adapt to Life in the United States.* New York City, NY: Russell Sage Foundation.

Chapter 4

The Hmong Culture

There is not an easy answer to the question of what constitutes the cultural identity of the Hmong people. Stereotypes of the Hmong as a group dates back to ancient Chinese times.

From as early as the twenty-seventh century B.C., the Hmong people appeared in Chinese history as the group of people who hindered the Chinese expansion into the basins of the Yellow and Hoia Rivers. Historically, the Hmong people were considered as inferior or barbaric by the Chinese. Strict measures were taken by the Chinese to divide, dominant, and conquer the Hmong and their lands (Lee, 1996).

Throughout history, the Hmong people have learned to adapt to their ever changing environment and still be able to maintain their unique sense of cultural and identity as a group. Unlike many immigrants and refugees arriving in the United States of America, the Hmong people were already considered a minority group within their own homelands and as a result, brought with them a distinctive sense of cultural identity (Quincy, 1997).

The earliest traces of the Hmong people were in the Kweichow Province of China, from where they moved and eventually spread out to Northern Vietnam, Thailand, and Myanmar (Burma).

The Hmong people are a mountain and agrarian group, preferring to build their home in the higher altitudes, usually above five thousand feet. Here, in their mountain environments, the Hmong people farmed using the slash and burn technique, which involved cutting and burning trees and vegetation into clear parcels of land, then fertilizing them. A major source of income for the Hmong villagers was the growing of opium, which they used as medicine and sold the rest to the Chinese.

Hmong farmers would raise pigs and chickens, oxen and horses, though few families were able to afford an ox and even fewer could afford a horse. Oxen served a dual purpose; they were used as work animals and for sacrifice at funerals. Horses were used for hauling and transporting. Pigs and chickens were the principle source of protein in the Hmong diet, but their main purpose was sacrificial. However, sacrifices were considered important to Hmong agrarian life, as the ancestors must be appeased and illnesses must be cured. Hmong villagers were willing to forego meat in their diet for several months if necessary (Quincy, 1997).

Sanitation in the Hmong villages were poor, however mortality rates were considerably low possibly attributed to the low consumption of alcohol and tobacco. Illness was believed to be caused by evil spirits and treatment for illness was offered by the Shaman, a religious person with duties similar to that of a physician and priest. When no cure was known, the Hmong villagers would turn to animal sacrifice and other religious rituals, such as wrapping fibers around the wrist to keep the soul in the body (Soua, 1998).

The term *Miao* was used in China to refer to the non-Chinese people of Southern China. Later, during the Tang and Sung Dynasties, the term *Nan Man*, meaning "Southern Barbarian" was used to describe the Hmong people. By 862 A.D., the word *Miao* reappeared once more in China. Today, the Hmong are referred to as *Miao Tseu* by the Chinese. This literally translates into "Sons of the Soil." There are approximately seven and a half million Hmong people around the world with more than three million living in China and Southeast Asia at this time (Lee, 1996).

A People on the Move

A common and accurate conception of the Hmong is that they are a people on the move. Every ten years, they are said to migrate to a different village after they have slashed and burned the forest around their old settlement. The Hmong people are not considered as permanent settlers and they have been known to move freely across borders between neighboring countries. The Hmong people are most largely found in Southern China, Vietnam, Laos, Thailand, and Myanmar (Burma) (Lee, 1996).

Up until a quarter of a century ago, Hmong was an obscure word used to describe a people who were virtually unknown in the Western world. This once unfamiliar people of the mountain regions of various Asian countries became the forefront of international migration due to their involvement and entanglement in the Vietnam Conflict. Occupying a strategic geographical location, the Hmong people served as a buffer zone against Communism in Laos (Lee, 1997).

Awareness of the Hmong as an ethnic group in the United States of America has not necessarily meant an understanding of the people and the culture. Often confused with Cambodians, Laotians, and Vietnamese people, the Hmong have migrated to the United States in large numbers over the past twenty-five years with little research available that examines this unique Asian group.

According to Gordon (1982), one of the biggest obstacles in research on ethnic groups is the lack of theoretical integration. Gordon believed that the little knowledge that does exist on ethnic groups is poorly articulated, making it difficult to derive a hypothesis that would guide the research process. Gordon went on to state that much of the limited research available in the area of ethnicity is atheoretical in nature and is not derived from theory nor does little to contribute to theory building most of the time.

The Resettlement of the Hmong

A large proportion of Hmong people resided in refugee camps in Thailand for most of the 1970's and well into the 1980's. Their conditions were harsh for months at a time, and for many, even years, were spent waiting for resettlement.

Unlike the Vietnamese that were evacuated by the Americans early in 1975 to arrive in the United States, the Hmong people did not earn this privilege until December of 1975. During this time period, the United States Congress admitted 3,466 Hmong people.

In May of 1976, another eleven thousand Laotians were granted entry into the United States of America, although there was no information given on the ethnicity of these allowed groups. In August of 1977, the United States Congress paroled some eight thousand "land people" most of which came from Laos.

By the early 1980's, approximately fifty thousand Hmong people had been resettled in the United States. The number of Hmong people residing in the United States of America had reached one hundred thousand by the 1980 census (Chan, 1994).

Approximately half of the Hmong in Thailand refugee camps made the decision to migrate to western countries rather than to remain in the camps until it might one day be safe to return to their homelands. Several thousand Hmong resettled in the countries of France, Australia, and

Canada, but the majority chose to resettle in the United States of America. Churches and small community groups were the first to sponsor the initial wave of Hmong families into the United States. Soon, the new Hmong refugees became sponsors themselves and a large wave of Hmong people came after the first wave of refugees became United States citizens (Quincy, 1997).

Since 1975, the United States of America has accepted over 110,000 refugees that were identified as Hmong or Laotian Highlanders. As a people who trace their ancestry back to China some thousands of year ago, it is an understatement to say that the Hmong people have experienced cultural shock in their resettlement to the United States. With horrid memories of the East Asian Wars and life in the refugee camps, the Hmong people have found themselves placed in a highly industrialized and technologically driven society.

The Hmong people have experienced linguistic, educational, economical, cultural and racial barriers since moving to the United States. Most Hmong did not even live in urban or industrialized cities or in homes where there was indoor plumbing and electricity prior to life in the United States. The Hmong's traditional values of family and group welfare above all else are in direct conflict with the American values of individualism and self-determination (Pfaff, 1995).

The Hmong people have suffered from years in war torn Asia and the resulting political upheaval. The stress resulting from this has compounded the migration strain that all immigrants in the United States of America experience. Many refugees have experienced unwilling separations and long-term exposure to countless traumatic events, while fleeing their homeland, residing in refugee camps, and eventually migrating to the United States.

Many Hmong refugees have been placed in strange and unpredictable environments. In addition to language barriers and experiencing homesickness, they have had to make the adjustment to physical, economic, religious, educational, value orientations, political, and social relationship changes within the United States.

For many Hmong families, there was a sudden lack of extended family relationships and community support upon immigration to the United States in a time when it is most essential to proper functioning. When the stressors are extreme and support systems along with the old ways of coping are lacking, refugee families in cultural transition frequently cannot adapt to the necessary environmental changes.

Adjustment to the host culture is a prolonged developmental process that affects each family member differently, depending on the individual and the family life cycle phase they are in at the time of transition. Individual family members within one household frequently will differ in their rate of acculturation. The degree of acculturation depends greatly on the years the refugee family has resided in the United States of America, the age at the time of migration, exposure to the Western culture and people, formal and informal affiliations and alliances, work and educational environment, and English speaking capabilities (McGoldrick, Giordano, and Pearce, 1996).

Hmong in the United States of America

According to Sucheng Chan (1994), it is nearly impossible to generalize how well the Hmong people as a group have adjusted to life in the United States of America because their conditions in different regions of the country vary a considerable amount.

The approximately 300,000 Hmong people who reside in the United States span from the East to the West coast with the largest populations residing in Wisconsin, Minnesota, and California (St. Olaf, 1997). Over 20,000 Hmong people migrated to Minnesota from California in 1998 alone. There is currently an estimated 50,000 Hmong refugees currently residing in the state of Minnesota (Lao Human Rights Council, 1998).

Many of the Hmong people living in the state of Minnesota are refugees, and adjustment to life in the Midwest has been trying. The Hmong people have a 4,000 year old history in China, Laos, and other Asian countries. In the Laotian Mountains, the Hmong people farmed using water buffalo as work animals and hand tools for their daily work. They believed in the spirit world and spiritual possessions capable of altering the life course and health of an individual and they had no written language up until the 1950's.

In the 1970's, with the aftermath of the Vietnam Conflict, many Hmong people who had helped the United States government fight against the Vietnamese and Laotian Communist Regimes, sought refuge in the United States. By the end of the Vietnam Conflict, thousands of Hmong people were slaughtered in retaliation for helping the United States of America.

Currently, one of the largest populations of Hmong refugees has resettled in Minneapolis and St. Paul, Minnesota. In the twenty-five years since the first Hmong person had arrived in Minnesota, acculturation has been an unsettling process for all. The first Hmong people to arrive in Minnesota was in December of 1975 and by May of 1979 there were some 1,300 Hmong people living in Minneapolis and St. Paul (Taylor-Hayes, 1999).

Several experts have cited welfare changes in the states of California in the mid-1990's as a major reason many Hmong people left that state and migrated to Minnesota and Wisconsin. Vang Pobzeb, the Executive Director of the Lao Human Rights Council in Eau Claire, Wisconsin believes that many Hmong people have left California for Minnesota and Wisconsin since 1997, when welfare reform threatened to cutoff funds. But Minnesota welfare officials claim the movement of the Hmong people to the Midwest has not triggered a swelling in the state's welfare rolls. It is even argued that the federal time limits imposed on welfare recipients led the Hmong people to look for someplace where more entry-level jobs were available to them (Winona Daily News, 2001).

Currently, there are four regions of the United States of America with large clusters of Hmong people. Minnesota, Wisconsin, and Michigan have the largest groups of Hmong with about 81,000 total. The Pacific Coastal states are second with about 68,000, the Carolinas and Georgia are third with around 9,000 and Colorado, Kansas and Oklahoma are fourth with approximately 5,000 Hmong people in residence (Winona Daily News, 2001).

Hmong as a Culture

Hmong culture stems from a patriarchal system and is organized by group or clan. Traditional family roles have been defined through this patriarchal system and have remained stable throughout centuries due to relative isolation from the rest of the world.

Historically, the Hmong male has held the leadership roles for both home and community, as well as having the primary responsibility for raising sons. Hmong women remain silent in discussions and matters of governance within the clan. Hmong women are primarily responsible for childbirth, tending to the home, assisting in the fields, and teaching the traditions of the Hmong people to the children. Recent exposure to the United States and its culture, education for the Hmong, especially for females, and new opportunities for younger Hmong people has resulted in challenges both to the roles of the family and the politics of the clan (Miyares, 1998).

The Hmong social structure promotes family and the clan. A patriarchal system determines the clan fellowship, in which Hmong women, once married, become members of the husband's family. All members within the same clan, or with the same last name, even when there is no blood relationship, are forbidden to intermarry.

*The elder Hmong female is responsible for passing down
Hmong history, traditions, and culture to children.*

On the other hand, close family members are encouraged to intermarry their children so that the blood will stay in the family. Therefore, marriages between first and second-degree cousins are relatively common.

Kathleen McInnis (1991), examined the main purpose of the Hmong clan and the roles of Hmong clan leaders in the United States of America. McInnis found that the clan leader is important to the group as he serves as a chief of all families with the same last name and represents them all in interactions with persons outside the clan. The clan serves as reinforcement to the Hmong people's sense of belonging and serves as the means to individual problem solving and decision making. There are no explicit rules for leadership selection. Rather, the potential candidate for clan leader is recognized by other members of the group after he has accomplished considerable and valued work for the benefit of his clan.

The large migration of Hmong to Minnesota from California in 1998 is not a phenomenon that is easily explained. Cheu Thao, a Hmong writer (1998), believes there is a direct parallel between secondary migration in the United States of America and the Hmong people's tradition of moving from one place to another in response to adverse conditions.

Cheu Thao believes that the Hmong residing in the United States move either to reunify with clans, whose members may have become separated during the journey from Laos to Thailand and then to the United States, or to improve their lives through job opportunities, lower housing costs, larger public assistance payments, and higher numbers of clan members present. Cheu Thao believes that the Hmong clan leaders in the United States of America attempt to gather together in one locality as many of their members as possible in order to maintain their social standing and influence over the clan.

According to Sucheng Chan (1994), secondary migration of the Hmong people in the United States of America may also occur in order to increase the size of the Hmong within a community and also to maintain social relationships that form the basis of the Hmong ethnic identity. Members of self-contained communities do not need to interact as much with the Anglo world as they find companionship among their own clan members. Most importantly, in such a setting, the Hmong people can exert social control over their younger Hmong members with greater effectiveness.

Chan has analyzed various facets of the Hmong people' adaptation to the United States of America perhaps more thoroughly than any other researcher. She examined four pre-migration variables and five post-migration variables to assess the nature and degree of the Hmong people's acculturation in the United States.

The pre-migration variables studied by Chan were language, traditional occupations, war experience, and kinship based network of authority. The post-migration variables in Chan's study were settlement patterns, ethnic composition of the neighborhoods settled by Hmong, socio-economic status of the settlements, resources provided by the federal, state, and local governments to the Hmong refugees, and the values held by the host society.

Chan pointed out in her research that the Hmong people who arrived in the United States of America had already encountered many disruptions in their lives. During the Vietnam Conflict, most Hmong people had to abandon their agricultural lives in the mountains and become dependent upon American airdrops of food and other necessities while they resided in refugee camps in Thailand.

The Vietnam Conflict also left a significant social impact on the Hmong people. As men left home to become soldiers, the extended kinship network was weakened. Hmong families moved in large numbers to cities and metropolitan areas. For the first time in centuries of history, Hmong children where attending formal educational institutions.

Chan noted that after the Hmong arrived in the United States of America, they faced even greater changes within a material cultural system. These changes involved the ways in which people made a living, the social structure, religious practices, and leadership in communities. Most Hmong people in the United States no longer lived in extended families. American laws forbid too many people residing in a small residential apartment or home. Social service agencies also affect the Hmong people's concept of family as emphasis is placed on the nuclear family and not the extended family for services.

Resettlement to the United States of America has not necessarily been a solution for the Hmong people's problems. Hmong refugees have faced the tremendous task to acculturate from a rural to a highly technological society. This accelerated cycle of acculturation forms the basis for new challenges, difficulties, and crises to a people who did not possess the skills necessary to successfully deal with the change.

When the Hmong people left the refugee camps of Thailand, they did not expect to confront changes in how they cook, shop, and deal with financial matters. Beginning in the Spring of 1982, the Federal cash assistance for refugees under the Indochina Migration and Refugee Assistance Act was reduced from 36 to 18 months of financial benefits. Once the 18 months have passed, the refugees are left on their own to find new means of support. Thus, large groups of unemployed refugees have been compelled to turn toward public assistance programs. Many Hmong people have cited their lack of English speaking ability as a primary reason for difficulty while adapting to life in the United States (Reder, 1986).

"Honorable United States Government and her citizens. Hmong resettlement in the United States is not a simple problem that we can can solve after 18 months or within a few years. According to man's history of development, it took more than a century to become modern. Hmong, unlike other refugees, came to the USA with only their lives. Hmong did not have a chance to prepare themselves before they came. Hmong's cultural life is almost totally different from the western society. Why did the government give Hmong an incredible 18 month period to prepare a self-supported life in this modern Society?
(From a Hmong Refugee Resettlement, 1984).

Feagin and Feagin (1995), theorized that the relationship between a minority and a majority group can be highly exploitative. Minority group members are maintained at the bottom of the economic and social system where they are expected to serve the needs of the majority group. Feagin and Feagin termed this exploitation "internal colonialism".

Acculturation and assimilation are important in placing certain behaviors, such as the language spoken, how one dresses, what foods one eats, a person's name, and so forth, into a workable context. Each characteristic behavior may signal the extent to which an individual or a group wishes to identify or has succeeded in identifying with a particular cultural population and is labeled as a member of that group (Teske and Nelson, 1974).

Hmong refugees are a group which come from an age of war and international policy that has catapulted millions of people outside their home environments. Refugees are the human measurement of political stability, justice, and social order. The exodus of the Hmong people from Laos, Vietnam, and Thailand since 1975 is part of the rapid outgrowth of refugees in the twentieth century (Winter, 1993).

According to Roger Zetter (1988), the term "refugee" constitutes one of the most powerful labels currently in the repertoire of humanitarian issues, national and international public policies, and societal distinction. The term refugee is associated with some of the most disturbing human experiences known to mankind. Experiences such as genocide, dislocation, and disruption, forced migration, alienation, and significant losses.

The Training Center for Indochinese Paraprofessionals of Boston University (1982), presented the cultural adaptation model to use as an indicator on how a refugee might adjust to life in the United States of America by going through a series of defined stages.

The first two to four months, a new refugee might experience a honeymoon phase of adaptation, during which he or she may feel quite positive and optimistic about the host country. After the honeymoon stage, the refugee may go through a crisis period, in which he or she experiences problems with transportation, job training and skill, and adaptation to the new host environment. The refugee may feel extremely isolated, insecure, or even inadequate in the new socio-cultural environment. This period can last from six months to years, depending on the refugee's personality and personal experiences.

The final stage of adaptation involves the second generation, which relate to the negotiation and acceptance of the new host environment and culture. Development of a generation gap, role conflicts, or status changes can result during this final stage. Several years may pass before refugees may successfully exit this stage. Previous life experiences, educational level, and career development can influence the speed to which a refugee will adapt to the new host culture.

Rochester, Minnesota is a small city of some 72,000 people located 85 miles southeast of Minneapolis and St. Paul (United States Census, 2000). In the mid 1980's, there were less than 40 Hmong residing in Rochester with the vast majority of Hmong people living in Minneapolis and St. Paul (United States Census, 1990). By the time of the 1990 U.S. Census, there were 200 Hmong people living in Rochester, representing three percent of the total Asian population in Minnesota. The 2000 U.S. Census does not break down the Asian population figures by identification of the Hmong people, however, interviews with local area Hmong clan leaders estimate there are currently some 300 Hmong living in Rochester.

The increase in the Hmong population in the Rochester area has been one of concern to the local community. Within an adequate knowledge base of the Hmong people, psychologists, social workers, therapists, and other helping professionals may not be able to effectively help the Hmong community in overcoming the obstacles related to adaptation and acculturation in the Midwestern United States. The Hmong people are considered newer Americans and Midwesterners and as such are in need of support in order to become contributing members of the economic, social, political, and educational components of the host community.

To maximize productivity as new Americans, the Hmong people need to be provided equal opportunities for successful adaptation to the United

States of America. Within an adequate understanding of the needs of the Hmong people in Rochester, Minnesota, services and programs offered to this group will remain ineffectual. Posavac and Carey (1992), stated that when the needs or the context of a people in need are not assessed accurately or are only partially understood, programs and services to this group cannot be as efficient or as effective as desired.

Research on the .Hmong people of the Midwestern United States can serve as a knowledge base for helping professionals in understanding this population group and their specific and unique needs. It also serves as a foundation for workable strategies in response to those needs.

The research that is presented in this book provides a new awareness of the Hmong people residing in Rochester, Minnesota and their current state of adaptation and unique acculturation needs.

REFERENCES

Chan, S., (1994). *Hmong Means Free. Life in Laos and America.* Philadelphia, PA: Temple University Press.

Feagin, J., and Feagin, C., (1995). *Racial and Ethnic Relations (5ᵗʰ Ed.).* Englewood Cliffs, NJ: Prentice-Hall Publishing.

Gordon, M., (1982). *Assimilation in American Life.* New York City, NY: Oxford University Press.

Hmong Moving Eastward: Census Data Show Heart of Hmong Community Moves to Upper Midwest. (2001, August 16). The Winona Daily News. A1.

Lao Human Rights Council, (1998). 1998 Hmong National Population and Education Data in the United States. *Lao Human Rights Council.* [on-line]: Available: http://home.earthlink.net/~laohumrights/1998.data.html.

Lee, G., (1996). Cultural Identity in Post Modern Society. Reflections on What is a Hmong. *Hmong Studies Journal.* 1.1: pp. 4-10.

Lee, M., (1997). The Thousand Year Myth: Construction and Characterization of Hmong. *Hmong Studies Journal.* 2.1: pp. 1-7.

McGoldrick, M., Giordano, J., and Pearce, J., (1996). *Ethnicity and Family Therapy (2ⁿᵈ. Ed.).* New York City, NY: Guilford Press.

McInnis, K., (1991). Ethnic Sensitive Work with Hmong Refugee Children. *Child Welfare League of America.* 5.60: pp. 571-579.

Miyares, I.M., (1998). *The Hmong Refugee Experience in the United States.* New York City, NY: Garland Publishing, Inc.

Pfaff, T., (1995). *Hmong in America: Journey from a Secret War.* Eau Claire, WI: Chippewa Valley Museum Press.

Posavac, E., and Carey, R., (1992). *Program Evaluation.* Englewood Cliffs, NJ: Prentice Hall Publishing.

Quincy, K., (1997). *Hmong: History of a People.* Seattle, WA: University of Washington Press.

Reder, S., (1986). *Hmong Resettlement Study.* Minneapolis, MN: Southeastern Asian Refugee Studies of the University of Minnesota.

St. Olaf University, (1997). *Hmong and Immigration: Frequently Asked Questions* [on-line].Available: http://www.stolaf.edu/people/cdr/hmong/faq/

Soua, T., (1998). *The Hmong Faced to the Western World. A Historically Unprecedented Attempt to Achieve a Century of Evolution within a Decade.* [on-line]: Available: http://www.hmong.com/the/essays/thesis/rs0001a.htm.

Taylor-Hayes, K., *Tested by the Past: Torn by the Future.* (1999, February 26). The Minneapolis Star Tribune. A4-A8.

Teske, R., and Nelson, B., (1974). Acculturation and Assimilation: A Clarification. *American Ethnologist.* 1: pp. 351-367.

Thao, C., (1982). *The Hmong in the West.* Minneapolis, MN: University of Minnesota Press.

The Training Center for Indochinese Paraprofessionals, (1982). *A Mutual Challenge: Training and Learning with the Indochinese in Social Work.* Boston: MA: Boston University School of Social Work.

U.S. Census Bureau (1991). *USGS Geographic Names Information System.* [on-line]. Available: http://www.census.gov/cgi-bin/gazetteer.

U.S. Census Bureau (2000). *American Fact Finder Census.* [on-line]. Available: http://factfinder.census.gov/servlet.

Winter, R., (1993). *The Year in Review, World Refugee Survey.* Washington, DC: U.S. Committee for Refugees.

Zetter, R., (1988). Refugees and Refugee Studies. A Label and an Agenda. *Journal of Refugee Studies.* 1.1: pp. 1-6.

Chapter 5

Methodology

Overview

The research relationship that is created in a qualitative study is conceptualized as gaining entry or establishing rapport with the research participants. The relationship is often complex and changes over time. In the qualitative study, the researcher is the instrument of the research and the research relationship is the means by which the research is completed. This relationship not only has an affect on the participants within the study, but on the researcher as well, and on other parts of the research's design (Maxwell, 1996).

Qualitative research methods allow the researcher to be more spontaneous and flexible in exploring phenomena in the participants natural environment (Rudestam and Newton, 1992). Qualitative methods are particularly useful in the generation of categories for understanding human beings, human experiences, and the investigation or the interpretation and meaning that people give to events they experience (Rudestam and Newton, 1992). Therefore, the researcher using qualitative methods seeks a psychologically rich, in-depth understanding of individuals or phenomenon that occur in people's lives.

Qualitative methods share three fundamental assumptions: 1. A holistic view which seeks to understand phenomena in their entirety in order to develop a complete picture of understanding about people, programs, or situations and events; 2. An inductive approach in which the researcher does not impose much of an organizational structure or make assumptions about the interrelationships among the data prior to making the observations and; 3. Naturalistic inquiry or the use of a discovery oriented approach in the participant's natural environment (Rudestam and Newton, 1992).

Restatement of the Problem

The purpose of this research was to record some of the recollections of the Rochester, Minnesota area Hmong people and their process of migration into the Midwestern United States. This research examined the degree to which the Hmong people maintained their cultural identity and the level of Anglo conformity that was established since arrival in the United States.

This study explored the following research questions: *What effect does non-voluntary migration have on the acculturation levels as measured by cultural awareness and ethnic loyalty of the Hmong people in Rochester, Minnesota?*

Specific research questions that guided this study were as follows: *How do the Hmong people perceive their host Anglo cuture? How do the Hmong people adjust to their host social system within the United States of America? How much do the Hmong people learn about their new environment? How do the Hmong people retain their traditions within the United States of America?*

These questions were studied and addressed in order to build a knowledge base about Hmong refugees and their unique cultural identity and acculturation needs. This knowledge base about the Hmong people of Rochester, Minnesota can be utilized to formulate workable strategies in responding to their unique needs and to empower the Hmong people to become active members of the greater Rochester community.

Research Expectations

This study was expected to result in an increased understanding of the Hmong refugees who have chosen to migrate to the Midwestern United States. This study sought to understand the Hmong refugee migration experience and the reasons why some Hmong people have chosen to migrate from other states such as those who have come from California to Minnesota in large proportions in recent years.

This research examined levels of adaptation for the Hmong people to their new lives in Minnesota as it interplay's with one's awareness of the American Midwestern culture and the Hmong people's interest in maintaining their own sense of cultural identity.

This study examined the specific adaptation levels and needs of the Hmong refugee population. The results desired from this study were to provide a foundation for additional research of the Hmong people and the capacity of the Midwestern United States to effectively address adaptation issues related to this population and refugees in general.

Description of the Research Design

Design in qualitative research is an iterative process that involves what Maxwell (1996), terms "tacking" or the back and forth process between the different components of the design. Tacking involves assessment and the validity threats of the purpose, theory, research questions, and methods.

A conceptual framework explains either graphically or in narrative form, the key factors, constructs, or variables to be studied and the presumed relationships that occur among them. Conceptual frameworks are the researcher's current maps of the environment that is being investigated (Miles and Huberman, 1994). What this means is that the framework of the study evolves over time as the data is collected and information develops.

Phenomenological Perspective

This study approached the research questions from a phenomenological perspective. The phenomenological perspective seeks to understand the life experiences of the individual participants and their intentions within the world that surrounds them. A phenomenological perspective seeks to answer the question: *What is it like to have a certain type of experience?* (Crabtree and Miller, 1992).

Through qualitative research approaches, the researcher is able to understand key processes of diverse family dynamics (Daly, 1992). These key processes include, intergenerational relationships, gender issues, and human development across the lifespan. Life course and gender researchers advocate the use of qualitative methodologies (Bengtson and Allen, 1993).

Ethnogerontologists are strong advocates in the use of varied qualitative methodologies, including the use of in-depth approaches to study the lives of ethnic minorities, refugees, and immigrant group members (Barresi, 1987). Barresi (1987), suggested the use of qualitative methods such as semi-structured interviews for research with multicultural groups.

Qualitative researchers focus on highlighting the heterogeneity of people's lives rather than on reporting averages or means that flatten the experiences of those persons who fall on either end of the spectrum. Qualitative measures serve to enhance the data presented in research and to illustrate the wide variety of human experiences found in different ethnic minority members.

Through the use of qualitative methods, psychologists, social workers, therapists, and other helping professionals, dynamically highlight the features and attributes of the participants within their own unique social context.   With intergenerational family contexts, qualitative researchers are able to examine the unique attributes of individual members within a family and within the confines of the home or natural environment.

By describing behavioral patterns, rituals, traditions, and other cultural phenomenon that are often undetected through quantitative measures, the qualitative researcher captures family and group processes, variations within and between family members, and explores the interplay between retaining one's ethnic identity and the cultural awareness one has about the host environment.

Qualitative research begins with foreshadowed problems that are anticipated as research questions that are initially formulated and then reformulated during data collection.   The continual reformulation of the research questions is expected as data collection strategies acquire a more holistic and total picture of the participants within the study, which results from an emerging research problem (McMillian and Schumacher, 1997).

The role of the researcher in this qualitative design is that of interviewer and observer-participant. For the purpose of this study, the interview role was outlined in the guide of questions found in Appendix A. The role of observer-participant versus being a participant-observer was chosen in this study in order to show a more focused intent upon observations of the Hmong people in their natural environment with less focus on the participatory role.

Observer-participation allows the researcher to become part of the natural environment and to develop a relationship and rapport with the participants being studied. When observing, researchers see first hand how the actions of the participants correspond with the interview questions and data. In writing about observation, Stakes (1995), notes that qualitative researchers should not confine themselves to interpretations or the identification of variables and development of instruments before data gathering occurs. Analysis and interpretation of the research should be withheld until the research data is complete.   The researcher should conduct fieldwork in the form of observations to objectively record what is occurring. During the observation process, the researcher simultaneously finds reasons for what is happening and then redirects the observations to refine or substantiate those suppositions.

Just as an archeologist reconstructs life forms from historical documentation, the qualitative researcher corroborates observations and interviews with document analysis. Documents provide the researcher with historical and demographic data as well as personal information that is often times unavailable from other sources of information.

Lincoln and Guba (1985), provide an outline of a broad series of ten design considerations that describe what should be considered by the qualitative researcher in advance, in preparation of a naturalistic study. The first three design considerations pay explicit attention to the assumptions that underlie a qualitative study and the fit of those assumptions to the method used.

Lincoln and Guba's (1985), design considerations include the following: 1. Determine a focus for the inquiry; 2. Determine the fit of the paradigms to the focus; 3. Determine the fit of the inquiry paradigm to the substantive theory selected to guide the study; 4. Determine where and from whom the data will be collected; 5. Determine successive phases of the inquiry; 6. Determine instrumentation that will be used; 7. Plan data collection and methods for recording; 8. Plan data analysis procedures that will be used; 9. Plan the logistics of the operation and; 10. Plan for trustworthiness.

Operational Definition of Variables

This study utilized a correlational method, which relies on careful observation of the participants within their own natural setting. The correlational method relies on recording and classification of behaviorism's in order to determine relationships between the variables. The correlational method is most often used when manipulation of variables is not possible for practical and ethical reasons. For the purposes of this research, operational definitions of the variables within the research questions are provided below.

Non-Voluntary Immigrant: A person who immigrates because he or she is unable to remain or return to his or her country of origin due to possible persecution or a well-founded fear of persecution based on one's race, ethnicity, nationality, religion, membership within a particular social group, or political ideology (Haines, 1996). Non-voluntary immigrants are also referred to in this study as refugees.

Ethnic Loyalty: The degree to which a person maintains the attributes from his or her culture of origin while residing as a minority in another country. These attributes include: language, religious beliefs and practices, availability and suitability of employment, family structure and dynamics, cultural holidays and traditions, level of education necessary for survival.

Cultural Awareness: The degree to which a person from a different culture than from where he or she currently resides understands and practices attributes attributed to the host or dominant culture. These attributes include: language, religious beliefs and practices, family structure and dynamics, type of work sought and attained, educational levels and importance of education, and the holidays and traditions observed.

Materials

Thirty-seven subjects in fifteen different Hmong families (Table 5.1) were interviewed using an interview guide with 145 questions that were designed by this researcher. The questions within the interview guide were structured and designed to lead the subjects into an in-depth discussion in the following categories: socio-demographic characteristics, housing, employment, family, health, social environment, maintenance of ethnic identification, understanding of the American culture, sponsorship, nutrition, and education. These questions were designed to encourage further responses by interviewer probing of the different categories in which family members experienced difficulties in individual interpretation and cultural adaptation.

Each participant was asked to sign an informed consent form (Appendix B) The consent form was read out loud to each participant and each participant was asked if they understood the contents of the informed consent form before signing. A Hmong translator, who was a bilingual specialist for the Rochester School District, was available at each interview for those subjects who had limited English speaking abilities or were more comfortable conversing in their native tongue.

Family members were notified that all information would remain anonymous and the participants were assured that they were free to decline from answering any question to which they were uncomfortable addressing. Subjects were provided with a detailed participant instruction page that described the purpose of the study, how responses would be used, and the extent of anonymity provided within the study.

Participants were contacted in person to conduct a short evaluation survey within two weeks after the completion of all the formal interviews. Participants were called upon by a Hmong speaking translator instead of the researcher for the evaluation survey to allow for freedom of expression in answering the questions. The surveys were anonymous and asked participants for their perceptions on the interview process with the researcher and perceptions about the interviewer. Participants were provided an opportunity to request information on the results of this research after completion without bearing a cost or obligation.

Table 5.1 – Gender by Household			
INTERVIEWED		**HOUSEHOLD**	
Family Male	Female	Male	Female
R01 3	1	4	4
R02 1	1	2	2
R03 0	3	0	3
R04 1	1	2	3
R05 2	1	6	8
R06 1	1	2	6
R07 2	2	5	9
R08 1	1	2	1
R09 1	0	2	5
R10 1	1	3	3
R11 1	1	2	2
R12 1	1	2	2
R13 1	3	2	3
R14 1	1	1	3
R15 1	1	3	4
Total 18	19	38	58

Selection of the Subjects

The research relationship that is created through the use of a qualitative study is conceptualized as gaining entry or establishment of rapport with the participants. The relationship is often quite complex and can change over a period of time. In the qualitative study process, the researcher is the instrument by which the research is completed.

The research relationship not only has an effect on the participants in the study, but also on the researcher and the other parts of the research design (Maxwell, 1996).

Gaining entry into a cultural environment other than that which the researcher is familiar and accepted is indeed a challenge. The process of developing relationships with potential Hmong subjects was enabled through a variety of means.

Discussion of the research question and the research process with Hmong people that the researcher had an established relationship. The researcher had a long-standing relationship with four Hmong people residing in the Southeastern Minnesota and Southwestern Wisconsin area. Three of the Hmong this researcher knew were prior college students at Winona State University and were majoring in Social Work. This researcher served as these Hmong students college instructor and faculty advisor during their undergraduate college years. All of these Hmong people have now graduated from the Social Work program and currently are working in social service settings throughout Southeastern Minnesota and Southwestern Wisconsin. The fourth relationship was developed between the researcher and a Social Worker at the Hmong Mutual Assistance Center of LaCrosse, Wisconsin. LaCrosse is a city of 52,000 people (LaCrosse Area Development Corporation, 2000) located approximately 75 miles east of Rochester, Minnesota and has a large Hmong population. All four of the above described Hmong persons were aware of this research project and were willing to assist in locating potential participants.

Attendance at Hmong cultural events. The Hmong people residing in Southeastern Minnesota and Southwestern Wisconsin offer several cultural events that are free and open to the public. The local Hmong clans have annual picnics, Hmong New Year celebrations, and cultural awareness events that the researcher had an opportunity to attend. In December of 1997, 1998, 1999, 2000, and 2001, this researcher attended the annual Hmong New Year celebration at the Olmsted County Fairgrounds in Rochester, Minnesota. Approximately 400 Hmong people attend this event in Rochester every year. The celebration offers an array of Hmong food, dancing, ceremonial dress, public forums, displays, and games. The researcher had the opportunity to meet the Rochester area Hmong Clan Leaders and respected Hmong elders at these events. This introduction was primary in receiving cooperation from the local area Hmong leaders to obtain necessary permission to do research with Hmong people as participants. Without this introduction, the research would never have been allowed to occur within the Rochester Hmong community.

Meeting with a Clan Elder. On April 1, 1999 a meeting with a local Rochester Clan Leader was scheduled with this researcher and a Hmong translator. Due to a death within the Clan Leader's family, the meeting was rescheduled with the second Clan Elder in charge of Rochester area Hmong affairs. Mr. Chang agreed to meet with this researcher and the Hmong translator in the evening hours of April 1, 1999. During a three hour discussion, this researcher explained to the Hmong Clan elder the purpose of the study and the researcher's intent to learn more about the Hmong people residing in Rochester, Minnesota. A formal request was made of the Hmong elder to grant this researcher the opportunity to interview 15 Hmong families in the Rochester area. Further, permission was requested to use my Hmong translator, a trained Social Worker and translator for the Rochester School District in the interview process. Mr. Chang agreed to both requests and stated he would be pleased to present his family as the first to be interviewed for the study.

This meeting with the Clan elder was necessary in order to gain entry into the Rochester Hmong community. Without seeking approval through the appropriate channels, this study would not have been possible, as Hmong families would have refused this researcher's request for an interview.

Only Hmong families residing in Rochester, Minnesota were selected to participate in this study. This study used purposeful sampling or criterion based sampling as a strategy for subject selection (Maxwell, 1996). This strategy was chosen because participants and sites were selected deliberately based on recommendations and referrals from interviewed subjects.

The sample size was fifteen multigenerational families and was based on availability and willingness of family members to participate. Thirty-seven participants from the fifteen families were interviewed ranging in ages from 13 to 80 years (Table 5.2).

There were four possible goals that were expected to be achieved by using purposeful sampling as a technique. The first goal was to achieve representativeness and typicality of the Hmong participants. The second goal was to adequately achieve the heterogeneity of the Hmong population to ensure that the conclusions adequately represented the range of variation. The third goal was to select a sample of Hmong people that deliberately examined cases that are critical to the theory within the study. The fourth goal was to establish particular comparisons of the Hmong participants to illuminate the reasons for differences between Hmong individuals (Maxwell, 1996).

Table 5. 2 – Subjects by Gender and Age

	INTERVIEWED		HOUSEHOLD	
Age	Males	Females	Males	Females
75-80	1	0	1	1
70-74	0	1	0	1
65-69	1	0	1	0
60-64	1	1	1	1
55-59	1	1	1	1
50-54	2	2	2	3
45-49	0	1	0	1
40-44	0	0	1	0
35-39	0	1	0	2
30-34	3	1	4	2
25-29	3	1	3	2
20-24	2	2	5	3
15-19	3	5	5	9
13-14	1	3	1	4
8-12	0	0	5	14
3- 7	0	0	7	8
1- 2	0	0	1	6
Total	18	19	38	58

It is important to keep in mind that the Hmong culture has changed since immigration to the United States. This is due to the length of time that the Hmong people have resided in the United States . Some Hmong people that were interviewed for this study were born in the United States of America and some of the subjects had completed a post secondary education, which is rare and unusual for the Hmong people in Asian countries. There were notable differences in religious practices of the Hmong participants and varied degrees of acculturation were found among members of the same Hmong household. To assist in establishing a positive research relationship, it was necessary to explain the purpose of the research project very clearly and decide what main points to communicate to different family members that were interviewed.

REFERENCES

Barresi, C.M., (1987). Ethnic Aging and the Life Course. In D.E. Gelfand and C.M. Barressi (Eds.). *Ethnic Dimensions of Aging.* New York City, NY: Springer Publishing Company.

Bengtson, V., and Allen, K., (1993). The Life Course Perspective Applied to Families Over Time. In P.G. Boss, W.J. Doherty, R. LaRossa, W.R. Schumm, and S.K. Steinmetz (Eds.). *Handbook for Family Theories and Methods: A Contextual Approach.* New York City, NY: Plenum Press.

Crabtree, B., and Miller, W., (1992). *Doing Qualitative Research: Research Methods for Primary Care, Volume 3.* Newbury Park, CA: Sage Publications.

Daly, K., (1992). The Fit Between Qualitative Research and Characteristics of Families. In J.F. Gilgun, K. Daly, and G. Handel (Eds.). *Qualitative Methods in Family Research.* Thousand Oaks, CA: Sage Publications.

Haines, D., (1996). *Refugees in America in the 1990's.* Westport, CT: Greenwood Publishing Company.

LaCrosse Area Development Corporation, (2000). *Welcome to Lovely, Lively LaCrosse.* [on-line]. Available: http://www.cityoflacrosse.org.

Lincoln, Y., and Guba, E., (1985). *Naturalistic Inquiry.* Thousand Oaks, CA: Sage Publications.

Maxwell, J., (1996). *Qualitative Research Design: An Interactive Approach.* Newbury Park, CA: Sage Publications.

McMillian, J., and Schumacher, S., (1997). *Research in Education: A Conceptual Introduction (4th ed.).* New York City, NY: Longman Press.

Miles M.B., and Huberman, A., (1994). *Qualitative Data Analysis: An Expanded Sourcebook.* Thousand Oaks, CA: Sage Publications.

Rudestam, K.E., and Newton, R., (1992). *Surviving Your Dissertation: A Comprehensive Guide to Content and Process.* Thousand Oaks, CA: Sage Publications.

Stakes, R., (1995). *The Art of Case Study Research.* Thousand Oaks, CA: Sage Publications.

Chapter 6

Research Procedures

The Hmong culture is one filled with rich tribal traditions and family rituals. In order for this researcher to establish a relationship that allowed for in-depth interviews with multigenerational Hmong families in the Rochester community, permission first had to be acquired from the Clan Leader of Rochester. Similar to a Human Subjects Review Committee, the Hmong Clan Leader read, reviewed, and discussed the research proposal before granting approval to proceed. The permission to conduct interviews with multigenerational Hmong families was granted in a formal discussion with the Rochester Hmong Clan elder on April 1, 1999.

Hmong families were acquired for this research using purposeful criterion based sampling technique. Hmong families that had consented and completed the interview process named referrals for possible Hmong participants to be interviewed.

Hmong participants were asked to review and sign an informed consent form before proceeding with the interview process. Hmong participants were interviewed in their family home environments to develop a higher comfort level during the question and answer process and to provide the researcher with the opportunity to observe Hmong participants within their own natural settings. The research interviews were recorded on a portable tape recorder and transcribed from the tapes verbatim. In the interviews where the Hmong translator was used, the translations from Hmong to English were transcribed from the tapes faithfully. Immediately following each interview, the researcher audiotape recorded necessary field observations and notes, as well as impressions of the process and what occurred during each interview.

Spradley (1979), recommends the qualitative researcher keep a journal during the data collection process. The journal should contain a record of the experiences during data collection, ideas, impressions, fears, mistakes, breakthroughs, misunderstandings and confusions, and the problems that arose during the data collection process. The qualitative researcher who keeps a journal of the experience is making an introspective record of fieldwork. This enables the qualitative researcher to take into account personal biases and feelings that intermingle with the research work, thus preventing these biases from potentially contaminating the work.

The interviews for this research were conducted with each family member in the household that was over the age of 13 years and expressed a willingness to participate. Hmong family members under the age of 13 years were not interviewed. This was to prevent potential changes within the family power structure and to provide more accurate responses to the questions provided during the interview.

Description of Instrumentation

The Hmong participants of this study were interviewed using a series of structured and semi-structured questions that were developed by the researcher. The questionnaire had several intended functions. 1. To provide structure, sequencing, and organization that ensured all the terrain was covered in the same order for each participant. 2. To establish channels for the direction and scope of the dialogue between researcher and participant. 3. To protect the larger structure and objectives set forth in the research process (McCraken, 1988).

The designed questionnaire, found in Appendix A of this book, was basically a structured interview schedule with close-ended and open-ended questions designed and intended to establish a dialogue with the Hmong participants.

The structure of the questions were formulated to lead into further discussion in the following categories: socio-demographic characteristics, housing, employment, family, health, social environment, sponsorship, nutrition, and education. The questionnaire was intended to encourage further response by the use of interviewer probing within the categories and to allow for accommodation when a participant experienced difficulty in interpretation and cultural adaptation.

The primary goal of the questionnaire was to allow for the Hmong participants to have flexibility in framing and structuring their responses through the use of semi-structured and open-ended questions. A fundamental component of qualitative research is that the phenomenon being examined must be told through the eyes of the participants and not the interpretations of the researcher (Marshall and Rossman, 1989).

The researcher in this study interviewed and observed three-generational Hmong families in order to achieve an understanding of Hmong culture and intergenerational experiences and differences. Interview questions were designed to maximize responses with the questions guiding the research intent carefully considered. This was accomplished through the use of major questions that included sub-questions in order to establish clarity of thought and specificity (Miles and Huberman, 1994).

The first objective of a qualitative interview is to allow the respondents to tell their own story in their own words and terms (McCracken, 1988). The use of open-ended questions helps the participants in the process of telling one's own story in his or her own terms. Semantic relationships were developed through the use of close-ended questions that were designed to seek clarification to the open-ended questions, but dealing with smaller units of specific experiences.

The Interviewing process was crucial to this research design in order to have a better understanding of past events that could not be observed, such as the Hmong participants explanation of how they arrived in the Midwestern United States. Observations helped to draw inferences about the Hmong participants meaning and perspective, particularly in areas the subjects were perhaps reluctant to discuss, such as, discriminatory experiences that have occurred since residing in the Midwest or in the United States of America.

Discussion of Data Processing

The approach to data analysis for this research was eclectic in that suggestions were borrowed from several qualitative research approaches. According to Brown and Gilligan (1992), and Miles and Huberman (1994), the techniques of listening to the voices of the participants and becoming immersed in the data collection is crucial in qualitative research to understanding the dynamics of each particular case before proceeding to cross examine case explanations.

Strauss (1987), and Lincoln and Guba (1985), suggest that coding and recoding are complete in qualitative research when the analysis appears to have run its course or when all the incidents can be readily classified. Thus, categories become saturated and sufficient regularities emerge from the data. The saturation and regularities process method was used in this study as a guide for ending the data collection and analysis phases of the research.

Data was coded and analyzed in this study by using WinMax ® computer software. WinMax ® is specifically designed for qualitative research using the phenomenological perspective. WinMax ® can be used for grounded theory oriented code and retrieval analysis as well as the use of Boolean, proximity and semantic retrieval. WinMax ® is a Scolari software product that is available for sale in the United States by Sage Publications.

After the data was coded by standard qualitative research methods, issues and themes emerged. Data analysis is the process of making sense out of the collected data (Merriam, 1998). Providing more than just raw data, the interview process in qualitative research gives the researcher an opportunity to learn from what is not seen in observations. Qualitative researchers often feel exhilaration when interviewing subjects and are rewarded by meeting new people and coming to understand people that they thought they might not otherwise meet (Glesne and Peshkin, 1992).

Because questions used in qualitative studies are semi-structured and open-ended (Merriam, 1998), the qualitative researcher gathers information by asking for more details through clarification seeking, and asking for specific examples. Glesne and Peshkin (1992), recommend that probing in qualitative research work should take on numerous forms. Some of the suggested forms of probing are: silence, sound, acknowledgment, and additional questions. Well executed interviews in qualitative research provide valuable data for the study that would not otherwise be found in a quantitative research study.

Methodological Assumptions and Limitations

Current research in cultural psychology has underplayed the notion that one's culture plays an important role in influencing thought, actions, feelings, and perceptions. Research in cultural psychology has shown favor to interpretation that the psychological phenomenon under study is shaped by culture and hence varies within and across cultural boundaries (Heine and Lehman, 1998).

Given that many psychological studies have emerged from within the Western Hemisphere and its dominant paradigm of individualistic views, researchers in this arena have developed limited findings with incomparable results when studying individual-based psychological processes within the eastern cultural view of collectivism.

One method of reducing this reoccurring and problematic culture bias in western research methodologies is to explore targets of evaluation that are more meaningful to the eastern cultures and ways of thought. In contrast to the individualistic views of self that is so common in the western cultures, the eastern cultures are characterized by a view of self that encompasses the important groups to which a person belongs or identifies (Heine and Lehman, 1998). Accordingly, the Hmong population that was studied included the individual Hmong as a member of a larger collective group of Hmong.

Several cultural differences between the researcher and the participants can potentially contaminate the research. Since the Hmong as a group were studied, the following cultural nuances were considered by the researcher.

The word yes does not always mean yes to a Hmong person. Yes may actually mean, "Yes, I respect that you asked a question," and not necessarily mean yes to the content of the question asked. No is considered disrespectful and a Hmong person may answer yes to a question even when that is not what is meant. Answers to questions by Hmong participants in the affirmative need to be reframed several times in different questions to give the Hmong person a way to answer the questions without having to say no.

Hmong people are reluctant to ask questions and hence expect the researcher to explain completely and thoroughly. The Hmong people respect firmness and politeness. Hmong people will be shy in an interview and are apt to appear aloof or reserved. Specific questions are more likely to appropriate a response rather than sole use of open-ended questions (Lao Family Community, 1998).

Language is key in the transmission of one's culture and the Hmong people are no exception. It is important to note that a Hmong translator was used in the majority of the interviews that were conducted in this study. Language differences between the researcher and the participants could result in misperceptions and miscommunications that can potentially contaminate the study. It is particularly difficult when communication between researcher and participant are left in the hands of a translator. Therefore, selection of an experienced person, trained in the art of translation is essential.

The Hmong participants who were involved in this study cannot be considered representative of all Hmong persons who reside in the Midwest, the United States or elsewhere in the world. The data obtained cannot necessarily be generalizable to the population of all Hmong people. The sample size was not randomly selected, subjects were voluntary and a small sample size was studied in-depth. Every effort was made to describe the sample used demographically and whenever possible, compare the

Hmong participants to other Hmong people within the Midwestern United States.

Reliability and Validity of Phenomenological Research

In traditional empirical research, the importance of reliability and validity are very important. Qualitative research also needs to carefully address the issues of reliability and validity. Be that as it may, traditional definitions of reliability and validity can create complications in qualitative studies. The corresponding terms for reliability and validity in naturalistic inquiry are more appropriately referred to as: 1. Auditability; 2. Credibility and; Fittingness (Guba and Lincoln, 1981).

Reliability is concerned with the replication of the study by a different researcher and under similar circumstances. The naturalistic inquiry researcher derives consistency through coding of the raw data in ways that another investigator could understand and replicate under similar circumstances. This is accomplished through the use of themes or concepts.

In the naturalistic inquiry process, credibility or truth is attained through structural corroboration. Such corroboration might be accomplished by the spending of sufficient time with the participants to monitor for distortions of information. This is referred to as prolonged engagement. Further, the qualitative researcher should explore the participants' experience completely and in sufficient detail. This is known as persistent observation. The qualitative researcher continues with this corroborative process by checking out multiple sources for information such as other investigators work, written records, diaries, field notes, and the like. This entire corroborative process is referred to in qualitative research as triangulation (Rudestam and Newton, 1992).

For the purposes of this study, the following methods of triangulation were followed: persistent observation, checking multiple resources for data and information, a comprehensive review of literature on the subject, and audio recording of interviews and field notes.

Consistent with qualitative methods, triangulated data for this research study was collected in several different forms: thirty-seven structured and open-ended, audio-taped interviews, five direct group observations of Hmong traditional celebrations, a complete and thorough review of the related literature, thorough discussions with Hmong community members and Clan Leaders, and as a final procedure, a focus group meeting that occurred several months after all the interviews were completed, transcribed and processed for analysis.

*The elderly are respected and revered by
many of the Rochester area Hmong.*

Generalizability of Phenomenological Research

External validity refers to the generalizability of the study. The emphasis of a qualitative study is a thorough and detailed description of a relatively small sample size of participants within the context of a specific and naturalistic setting. In the selection of participants for a qualitative study, the issue is sampling bias and not generalizability (Morgan, 1988). Making generalizations about other Hmong subjects or situations in this qualitative research are modest and mindful of the context of individual Hmong lives.

Phenomenological research uses sampling that provides a focus on the individual or case studied in order to understand the full complexity of the person or experience. Because phenomenological research has a foundation in this perspective, there cannot be an attempt to claim the ability to generalize to a specific population. However, the findings in phenomenological research are relevant from the perspective of the user of the findings (Morgan, 1988).

Credibility in Phenomenological Research

Wolcott (1990), presents nine points of credibility in qualitative research: 1. Talk a little and listen a lot. A sociable situation should exist where the participant feels comfortable discussing different topics with the researcher. The researcher needs to be attentive and responsive without speaking too much or hearing too little. 2. Record accurately. The researcher should make every attempt to record the participant's words precisely. Words should be recorded to prevent the reinterpretation of behavior as it is analyzed. 3. Begin the writing process early. The intent of writing early is to record what one suspects and to identify problems or gaps in the information provided. 4. Let the readers see the information for themselves. It is a good idea to include primary data in the final study allowing the expressed thoughts of others to become the point of focus rather than developing a focus on what the researcher observed and interpreted. 5. Report the information fully. Every discrepant detail is not necessarily reported, but if an issue is not fully resolved, the inclusion of such a discrepancy can lead to possible interpretations every bit as valid as the researchers. 6. Be candid and honest. Subjectivity is seen as a strength of qualitative research designs. 7. Seek feedback from others. Having a continual source of feedback is a good check for accuracy and completeness of work. Feedback provides a reality check where the reporting or the interpretation of the events needs to be more developed or is overblown and needs to be brought back to reality. 8. Try to achieve a healthy balance. Achieving a healthy balance between events that occurred or statements that were made is warranted in order to avoid a disproportionate amount of attention being given to outlying data. 9. Write the information completely and accurately. This process provides an opportunity to check for coherence and internal consistency, as well as for style and grammar.

Ethical Assurance

Every effort was made in this study to avoid harm to the participants. The Hmong subjects that participated in this research were not asked to do any activities that would place them at risk of harm. The research was conducted exclusively in the home of Hmong participants and involved asking a series of questions and observing the Hmong family in their natural environment.

Risk of harm to the participants was possible in that some of the questions that were asked in this study may have been uncomfortable or difficult to answer. The Hmong participants were asked to sign consent before proceeding with the interview process. With the informed consent, the Hmong subjects were made aware that some questions might be uncomfortable to answer and that an individual could decline to answer any question without explanation.

Finally, a post questionnaire was given within two weeks of the scheduled interview process and provided the Hmong participants an opportunity to share anonymously their feelings about the interview process as well as to request additional information or the results from this study.

REFERENCES

Brown, L., and Gilligan, C., (1992). *Meeting at the Crossroads: The Landmark Book about Turning Points in Girls' and Women's Lives.* New York City, NY: Ballantine Books.

Glesne, C., and Peshking, A., (1992). *Becoming a Qualitative Researcher.* White Plains, NY: Longman Publishing Company.

Guba, E., and Lincoln, Y., (1981). *Effective Evaluation.* San Francisco, CA: Jossey-Bass Publishing.

Heine, S., and Lehman, D., (1998). The Cultural Construction of Self-Enhancement: An Examination of Group Serving Biases. *Journal of Personality and Social Psychology.* 2.4 pp. 1-12.

Lao Family Community, of Minnesota, (1998). *About Lao Family Community of Minnesota.* [on-line]. Available: http://home.earthlink.net/~laohumanrights.

Lincoln, Y., and Guba, E., (1985). *Naturalistic Inquiry.* Thousand Oaks, CA: Sage Publications.

Marshall, C., and Rossman, G., (1989) *Designing Qualitative Research.* Thousand Oaks, CA: Sage Publications.

McCraken, G., (1988). *The Long Interview.* Thousand Oaks, CA: Sage Publications.

Merriam, S.B., (1998). *Qualitative Research and Case Study Applications in Education.* San Francisco, CA: Jossey-Bass Publishing.

Miles, M.B., and Huberman, A., (1994). *Qualitative Data Analysis: An Expanded Sourcebook.* Thousand Oaks, CA: Sage Publications.

Morgan, D.L., (1988). *Focus Groups as Qualitative Research.* Thousand Oaks, CA: Sage Publications.

Rudestam, K.E., and Newton, R., (1992). *Surviving Your Dissertation: A Comprehensive Guide to Content and Process.* Thousand Oaks, CA: Sage Publications.

Spradley, J.P., (1979). *The Ethnographic Interview.* New York City, NY: Harcourt Brance College Publishers.

Strauss, A.L., (1987). *Qualitative Analysis for Social Scientists* Cambridge, UK:. Cambridge University Press.

Wolcott, H.F., (1990). *Writing Up Qualitative Research.* Thousand Oaks, CA: Sage Publications.

Chapter 7

Demographics of Hmong People in Rochester

Overview

The qualitative research approach used in this study was designed to allow Hmong family members the occasion to openly portray their life experiences while residing in the Midwestern United States. The interview format utilized in this study gave Hmong family members the opportunity to describe personal and social experiences related to their adjustment in the United States of America, perspectives about their education and employment, experiences with discrimination, and the struggles associated with it.

This qualitative study also examined the loyalty of Hmong to their own culture and ethnicity, their perceptions and understanding of the American culture, and the meanings they attributed to being part of a minority group in Rochester, Minnesota.

While the process and preparation of qualitative research is often arduous and overwhelming, this particular approach provides the most appropriate framework for an in-depth analysis of the lives of Hmong people not readily obtainable in a quantitative study. Through interviews and participant observations, the meanings that the Hmong participants gave to their experiences while living in the United States contributed to a more richer and complex understanding of the reasons behind these families decisions to reside in Rochester, Minnesota.

Utilization of a qualitative research paradigm has several distinct advantages over a quantitative research model. One primary advantage of the qualitative research process is that it provides for a more holistic and developmental view of the Hmong participants' experiences, or more succinctly, the complex interactions of individuals in a cultural, sociological, psychological, and environmental state.   The end result is a better understanding of the affects the adjustment process has for the Hmong refugees.

A second advantage to the qualitative research paradigm is the opportunities that are available to be spontaneous and flexible within the interview process. This suppleness allows each Hmong participant the occasion to express and discuss his or her distinctive life experiences.

A third advantage in a qualitative research model is related to the importance of being empathetic, culturally sensitive, and responsive to each Hmong participant and his or her interpretation of what life is like within the Midwestern United States.   A final advantage is the wealth of information attained and the rich depth of each individual life story that is acquired through a qualitative research paradigm.

Qualitative research studies require an intensive involvement in the investigation process.   This includes a commitment of time and effort as well as coordination of the many overlapping and on-going aspects involved with this type of research process. The findings presented in this text are based on in-depth interviews with 37 Hmong participants from 15 Hmong families ranging in age from 13 to 80 years old.

Status in the United States of America

Thirty-seven Hmong persons in Rochester, Minnesota from   fifteen different multigenerational families were interviewed for this study.   The Hmong participants ranged in age from 13 to 80 years.   Eleven of the Hmong persons interviewed had attained citizenship status in the United States of America.   The remaining twenty-six subjects were permanent residents in the United States (Table 7.1).

There are eighteen total surnames in the Hmong culture, representing the eighteen Hmong family clans.   Eight of the family clans or surnames derived from the Hmong culture were represented in this study.   These families represented each of the Hmong surnames that were current residents in Rochester, Minnesota.

Four families came from the house of Chang, one from the house of Dher, one from the house of Gitter, two from the house of Her, three from the house of Lee, two from the house of Vang, one from the house of Xiong, and one from the house of Yang.

The Hmong families interviewed for this study were residing in the United States of America for a mean of 9.93 years. Eleven of the fifteen families had chosen Rochester, Minnesota as their city of destination in the United States.

Table 7.1 – United States Status				
Age	**Interviewed**		**Household**	
	Citizen	**Resident**	**Citizen**	**Resident**
75-80	0	1	0	2
70-74	0	1	0	1
65-69	1	0	1	0
60-64	0	2	0	2
55-59	1	1	1	1
50-54	1	3	1	4
45-49	0	1	0	1
40-44	0	0	1	0
35-39	1	0	2	0
30-34	3	1	3	3
25-29	2	2	2	3
20-24	0	4	0	8
15-19	2	7	4	10
13-14	0	3	1	3
09-12	0	0	19	0
03-08	0	0	14	1
01-02	0	0	7	1
Total	**11**	**26**	**56**	**40**

Life in Rochester, Minnesota

One of the Hmong families interviewed (R15) had originally arrived in Rochester, Minnesota upon coming to the United States of America but had later moved to Austin, Minnesota for three years. Austin is a city of 21,000 people and is located 45 miles west of Rochester, Minnesota (Austinmn.com, 2001). The mother of this Hmong family shared these comments regarding their return to Rochester, Minnesota:

*"We live for three years in Austin, Minnesota. We don't
like it there because there is no Hmong living there and
no Asian foods there, so we come back to Rochester."*

The remaining four Hmong families claimed residence in other cities
since arriving in the United States of America. Des Moines, Iowa; Sioux
City, Iowa; Green Bay, Wisconsin; St. Paul, Minnesota; Winona,
Minnesota; Austin, Minnesota; Sacramento, California; and Stockton,
California.

The Hmong families that participated in this study had resided in
Rochester, Minnesota for a mean of 8.33 years (Table 7.2). Some of the
reasons cited by the Hmong participants for choosing to live in Rochester,
Minnesota were: other family members who were residing in the city of
Rochester; a Rochester area Christian church that had sponsored Hmong
families from Thailand refugee camps to the United States; the small city
size of Rochester; and the overall low crime rate.

The city of Rochester is divided into four quadrants, which consist of the
Southeast, Southwest, Northeast, and Northwest sections of Rochester.
The Hmong families that were interviewed for this study were scattered
throughout the city of Rochester with no clearly defined "Hmong
neighborhood."

Six of the fifteen Hmong families resided in the Northeastern quadrant of
the city. Two of these six families identified one other Hmong family as
living within their defined "neighborhood". Five of the families
interviewed lived in the Southeastern quadrant of the city of Rochester.
Two of these families lived in the same mobile home park. Three of the
Hmong families that participated in this study were living in the
Southwestern quadrant of the city. One of these families lived in a rural
area outside of the city, quite a distance from the city's center. One family
lived in the Northwestern quadrant of Rochester and indicated that they are
not aware of any other Hmong families living within their neighborhood
(Table 7.3).

Four of the fifteen Hmong families interviewed were currently renting
their living quarters. One family was renting a single dwelling unit under
government subsidy for $135 per month. The other three Hmong families
who were renting their residences lived in multi-unit dwellings. The
lowest market-rate rent that was paid by a family was $250 per month.
The Hmong family paying the highest market-rate rent spent $540 per
month for a two bedroom unit.

Two Hmong families from this study had purchased older, single-wide mobile homes as dwellings. These two families paid cash for the mobile homes and a lot rent of $195 per month. The remaining nine Hmong families from this study were in the process of purchasing their own homes. All nine of these families resided in single dwelling units. The lowest mortgage payment spent by a family was $300 per month and the highest mortgage payment spent by a family was $1500 per month.

Some of the comments made by the Hmong participants of this study about residing in Rochester, Minnesota were as follows:

> *"I have traveled to other cities, but Rochester is the only place I ever lived. We live here because we had an Uncle here who sponsored us to come. Because we had our sponsor here, that is why we moved here. If we had sponsor in another city, perhaps, we live there now."*

> *"The Baptist Church in Rochester sponsored my family to come here. We like to stay in Rochester now because it is a clean city and low crime here."*

One of the Hmong participants described how the family came to live in Rochester. A relative who was then residing in the Midwestern United States sponsored the family:

> *"We didn't choose Rochester to live. We had a cousin who helped us and got the house we live in now. We just move here. We really want to move out, but it is too much money to move. That is why we keep living here."*

A Hmong family that moved from California to Rochester shared that they thought the job prospects for Hmong people would be better in Minnesota.

> *"Too many Hmong people live in California. The Hmong come to Minnesota for jobs. California has no money, no jobs for the Hmong people. Hmong come looking for work in Minnesota. My daughter moved here to Rochester when she got married. Now she moved to St. Paul. Too*

*big, too many people in St. Paul. I like it here. I am near
to the hospital, and I go to study school every day to learn
English. I like it here. I didn't like St. Paul."*

Table 7.2 – Years in the United States of America		
Family	**Years in the United States**	**Years in Rochester**
R01	11	11
R02	11	11
R03	6	6
R04	11	11
R05	19	12
R06	10	10
R07	5	2
R08	11	11
R09	18	4
R10	12	12
R11	14	14
R12	5	5
R13	4	4
R14	11	4
R15	11	8
Mean Years:	**10.33**	**8.33**

Of the fifteen families interviewed, fourteen were White Hmong. One
family was Striped Hmong. The father of the Striped Hmong family had
this to say about his identification with a Hmong clan.

> *"We are Striped Hmong people. For our people, we only
> have four kind of Hmong. My wife was a White Hmong
> and I was a Striped Hmong. This is only to identify the
> clothes that we wear. It doesn't really mean anything,
> it is only according to the Hmong clothes. It doesn't*

matter who marry who, for in our culture, the woman goes to the man's family and she start wearing their clothes. See, we go by the last name in Hmong. The Hmongs only have eighteen last names, like my name and my wife's name. When she marry, she became one of me and is no long a part of her family."

Table 7.3 – Hmong Neighborhoods of Rochester, Minnesota

Family	Northeast	Northwest	Southeast	Southwest
R01			X	
R02			X	
R03	X			
R04	X			
R05	X			
R06		X		
R07			X	
R08			X	
R09	X			
R10				X
R11	X			
R12	X			
R13			X	
R14				X
R15				X
Total	6	1	5	3

more important reasons for celebrating the Hmong New Year.

Country of Origin and Identification

A majority of the Hmong participants for this study and their family members were born in the country of Laos. One Hmong patriarch shared the history of his family's heritage and how they came to live in the country of Laos.

> *"We are from Laos. I was born in Laos, but my father's parents are from Peking in China. They moved to Laos with their family members many years ago. I can understand what the Chinese Hmong people are saying, but I don't speak the language. We, all the Hmong people, speak some Hmong, but we have different ways to speak it when we live in a different country."*

All of the Hmong families that participated in this study had spent a significant amount of time in the refugee camps of Thailand (Table 7.4).

The average length of stay in a Thailand refugee camp for the Hmong families interviewed for this study was six to seven years. There were a number of household members who were actually born in Thailand refugee camps. Further, the study revealed that some of the younger Hmong adults interviewed were born in Laos, but had little or no recollection of living there. These young Hmong adults are more likely to have strong ties and memories of their lives in Thailand.

A recently married, nineteen-year-old Hmong female that was interviewed shares that she was born in the country of Laos, but was an infant when her family fled that country. She identifies herself more as an American because, as she reports, this is the only place where she has a strong recollection of residing.

> *"I have traveled to many places. But I only really live here. I was born in Laos, but I was very little when we left. I cannot really tell you where Laos even is, as I was too young when we left there and I don't remember it. I lived in a refugee camp with my family in Thailand for two years. Now, this I remember very well."*

Some of the Hmong families interviewed had lived so long in Thailand that they had children born in the refugee camps. Other Hmong families had brought small children and infants to Thailand. These Hmong children with family origins to Laos have their cultural ties to Thailand and the United States but know nothing of their family's country of origin. A fifty-year-old Hmong male provided this perspective on the resettlement experiences of Hmong famillies.

> *"We had lived in a Thailand refugee camp for nineteen years. All my younger daughters were born in the country of Thailand. They have never been to our home in Laos. But for my wife and me, we are the only to remember Laos."*

Many of the families had children born in the United States as is noted by the length of time that these Hmong families have resided in the United States (Table 7.5). Within one of the families interviewed, the mother was Cambodian and married a Hmong male after they met in the United States of America. The remaining family members within this study were born in Laos, Thailand or the United States

Table 7.4 – Years Residing in Thailand	
Family	**Years**
R01	7
R02	10
R03	10
R04	9
R05	1
R06	1
R07	10
R08	2
R09	4
R10	6
R11	4
R12	10
R13	19
R14	4
R15	1
Median Years	**6.53**

One sixty-year-old male participant resided in his home in Rochester with three generations of his family. He shares that he is from the country of Laos, and some of his children were born in Laos. However, his younger children were born in Thailand during the family's ten-year stay in a Thai refugee camp. His older children, those born in Laos, are now married and have children of their own. Most of his grandchildren were born since the family has lived in the United States.

> *"I have come from Laos and my wife has come from Laos.*
> *My oldest sons, all three, were born in Laos. My other*
> *children were born in Thailand. My son's children, some*
> *were born in Thailand and some were born in the United*
> *States."*

A fourteen-year-old female Hmong participant shared with the researcher that her country of origin as Thailand. She recognized that her family is Hmong and that their country of origin is Laos, but she shared that she really knows nothing about the country of Laos, because she has never been there before. She sees herself as one day having children of her own who will become more like Americans than Hmong.

> *"I was born in Thailand, so I come from the country of*
> *Thailand. My mother and my father were born in Laos,*
> *So they come from the country of Laos. One day I will*
> *have children of my own and they will become Americans."*

Family Employment and Income

The Hmong families that participated in this study had a median family size of 6.4 people with a median gross income of $1822 per month (Table 7.6). Ten of the Hmong families (67 percent) interviewed received their monthly income from members of the family that were gainfully employed The majority of Hmong participants who held jobs were doing assembly line and factory type work.

One of the Hmong families interviewed had their own household business translating Asian acquired videos into the Hmong language for distribution and sale. Three families (20 percent) received their monthly household income from government disability or SSI payments and one Hmong family (13 percent) was receiving Temporary Assistance to Needy Families (TANF).

Table 7.5 – Country of Origin						
Family	**Interviewed**			**Household**		
	Laos	**Thailand**	**U.S.**	**Laos**	**Thailand**	**U.S.**	**Cambodia**
R01	1	3	0	3	3	2	0
R02	2	0	0	2	0	2	0
R03	2	1	0	2	1	0	0
R04	2	0	0	4	0	1	0
R05	1	0	2	3	0	11	0
R06	2	0	0	4	1	3	0
R07	3	1	0	5	6	3	0
R08	2	0	0	3	0	0	0
R09	1	0	0	1	0	5	1
R10	2	0	0	2	0	4	0
R11	2	0	0	3	0	1	0
R12	2	0	0	2	1	1	0
R13	2	2	0	3	2	0	0
R14	1	1	0	1	1	2	0
R15	2	0	0	3	1	3	0
Totals	**27**	**8**	**2**	**41**	**16**	**38**	**1**

Sharing the Findings – Themes and Dimensions

The questionnaire that was designed for this study was organized in a developmental fashion, from gathering of demographic data and family information, to collection of information on housing, employment, and language acquisition, to ethnic preservation and cultural identification.

All interviews were audiotape recorded and transcribed verbatim. Coding of transcribed interviews was completed by using WinMax sofware ® as a coding and analysis tool.

Miles and Huberman (1994) recommended organizing codes from qualitative studies into themes or categories with the goal of seeking patterns in the data. Although the questionnaire for this study was designed in a developmental and progressive fashion, the themes were allowed to emerge in an inductive fashion. No prior assumptions were made about the interrelationships among the data prior to the observation and analysis process.

Table 7.6 - Income by Household			
Family	**Monthly Income**	**Source of Income**	**Family Size**
R01	$1500	Employment	8
R02	$1200	Employment	4
R03	$ 850	Disability	3
R04	$ 740	Disability	5
R05	$4000	Home Business	14
R06	$1100	Employment	8
R07	$4000	Employment	14
R08'	$1200	Employment	3
R09	$3500	Employment	7
R10	$2500	Employment	6
R11	$2500	Employment	4
R12	$1600	Employment	4
R13	$1300	Employment	5
R14	$ 600	TANF	4
R15	$ 740	Disability	7

In order to provide the reader with a coherent and logical pattern or flow to the presentation of these findings, each of the four themes presented will be followed by an short analysis of the dimensions and data. A final analysis of the complied data will weave the themes and dimensions together into the logical pattern that will be presented following the discussion chapters of each of the four themes.

For the purposes of discussion and analysis, the Hmong participants will be referred to as Older Hmongs (ages 80-50 years); Young Adult Hmongs (ages 49-21years); and Pre-Adult Hmongs (ages 20-13 years) referred to in Table 7.7.

Table 7.7 – Subjects by Generation and Gender				

Age	Male	Female	Percentage
80-50	6	5	30%
49-21	8	6	38%
20-14	4	8	32%
Totals	18	19	100%

During the analysis of the data, four dominant themes emerged from the interviews. These themes were: 1. Awareness of Cultural Surroundings; 2. Loyalty to Ethnicity and Culture; 3. The Hmong Migration Experience; and 4. Religious and Spiritual Identification (Table 7.8).

The Hmong participants revealed some interesting language barriers that ultimately resulted in communication obstacles and difficulties in intergenerational relationships between grandparents, parents, and children. Family members shared their loyalty to the Hmong culture through the retention of traditions and holidays. Of particular emphasis were Hmong celebrations, clan gatherings, and Hmong holidays.

The Hmong families that participated in this research discussed ways in which their culture is lived and shared within the household as well as how American values and beliefs have become incorporated into the family and the household. Additionally, it was noted that the experience of each family's migration to Thailand and ultimately the United States of America, was a particular source of stress and in due course a struggle for all participants.

Quite unexpected, was the fourth theme that emerged through the interview process and this pertained to the concept of religions and spirituality for the Hmong. The emphasis in this theme was the role that religion and spirituality have played traditionally for the Hmong people and the role that religion and spirituality play for the present day Hmong family residing in the Midwestern United States.

Table 7.8 – Themes and Dimensions	
Themes	**Dimensions**
Awareness of Cultural Surroundings	Ability to Speak in English Education Levels Employment Health Care Family Relationships Integration in Community
Loyalty to Ethnicity and Culture	Retaining Hmong Language Hmong Traditions Family Structure
The Hmong Migration Experience	Post War Stress Refugee Experience Prejudice
Religious and Spiritual Identification	Traditional Religion Christian Influences

References

Austinmn.com (2001). *Living or Moving to Austin? Here is What We Have to Offer.* [on-line]. Available: http://www.austinmn.com.

Miles, M.B., and Huberman, A., (1994). *Qualitative Data Analysis: An Expanded Sourcebook.* Thousand Oaks, CA: Sage Publications.

Chapter 8

Theme One – Cultural Awareness

The theme of cultural awareness has several major dimensions associated with it. First of all, I will provide examples of differences in the abilities to speak English by the Hmong participants of this study.

Older Hmong participants reported a number of obstacles and difficulties in communicating with their children, employers, neighbors, and the community at large. The younger Hmong participants expressed fewer difficulties in communicating and negotiating within the Rochester community because of their higher comfort levels and mastery with the English language.

This difference in the mastery of the English language by older Hmong and younger Hmong participants resulted in greater misunderstandings between the younger Hmong and their parents and grandparents. Mastery and comfort levels in speaking English affected all dimensions of cultural awareness and is noted throughout the findings of this research.

The dimensions of education and employment were distinctly tied together for the participants of this study. Many of the Hmong participants who were born in Laos had acquired a very limited formal education, which affected their current and future employment possibilities.

Younger Hmong participants were more likely to have completed some form of formal education within the United States of America. However, at a young age, these Hmong participants were expected to work part-time while going to school in order to contribute to their family's meager income.

The Hmong participants understanding of how and when to use the various types of community services was quite limited by the majority of the families that were interviewed. This lack of understanding of the community resources correlates with the low frequency of usage of medical, dental, vision, and mental health care across all of the Hmong families that were interviewed.

English Speaking Abilities

The Hmong participants for this study had discussed at great length and at different times during the interview process the obstacles that occurred in the relationships of parents and children.   These obstacles were frequently cited as communication problems and language barriers. Many of the younger Hmong felt the most comfortable conversing in English while the older Hmong were much more comfortable speaking in their native tongue and expressed great hardship in learning to speak English (Table 8.1).

There was a great deal of diversity that existed in the preferred languages both in and between parents and their children and even from sibling to sibling. All of the older Hmong reported having the greatest comfort level in speaking their native language of Hmong. This was quite different from the reports of the younger Hmong and children who expressed a greater comfort level speaking in the English language.

The older Hmong that were interviewed recognized that their children's English speaking ability was far superior to their own. For many of the younger Hmong family members, English was the preferred language as they spoke it most frequently at school and work.   Some of the middle school aged Hmong children within the families interviewed did not speak or understand Hmong at all.   This created further communication and cultural gaps between the younger and the older Hmong.

This 55-year-old father expressed his belief that his children's English speaking ability is far greater than his own is.   He also believes that speaking in the English language results in having an understanding of the American culture.

> *"I think that my children know English better than they do Hmong language. I know maybe ten percent of English.   Our children and our grandchildren are speaking more in English.   They know more about this country than I do."*

Many of the older Hmong participants relied upon their adult children to serve as translators when speaking with their grandchildren who did not speak or understand Hmong. Although all the families that were

Table 8.1 – Language Preference

Family	Age	Gender	Percentage English	English Preference
R01	55	M	10%	No
	18	M	60%	Yes
	15	M	70%	Yes
	14	F	70%	Yes
R02	25	M	95%	Yes
	23	F	40%	No
R03	50	F	1%	No
	19	F	40%	No
	14	F	70%	Yes
R04	76	M	1%	No
	74	F	5%	No
R05	34	M	50%	No
	17	M	90%	Yes
	15	F	95%	Yes
R06	68	M	5%	No
	58	F	5%	No
R07	60	M	2%	No
	53	F	1%	No
	21	M	45%	No
	15	F	85%	Yes
R08	21	M	60%	Yes
	19	F	80%	Yes
R09	31	M	85%	Yes
R10	31	M	80%	Yes
	30	F	80%	Yes
R11	26	M	70%	Yes
	23	F	70%	Yes
R12	25	M	10%	No
	26	F	30%	No
R13	50	M	5%	No
	49	F	5%	No
	15	F	10%	No
	13	F	90%	Yes
R14	61	F	20%	No
	14	M	70%	Yes
R15	52	M	1%	No
	36	F	50%	No

interviewed expressed a desire to teach the younger generations in the Hmong language, this was not always the case.

This 76-year-old grandfather expressed that his children and his grandchildren were learning English at a rapid pace and that their ability to understand English was at such a rate that he believed he would never be able to catch up with them.

> *"I think that the children learn English faster than they do Hmong. They don't want to speak to us in Hmong, they want to speak to us in English. This is difficult for us as we don't speak English, it is so hard to learn for us."*

All of the Hmong participants of this study believed that their young children would become more American than Hmong. This was accepted by most older Hmong as a natural process and a desirable occurrence. The 23-year-old mother of a newborn child was very much aware of this and expressed the importance of her daughter's ability to learn English, not Hmong, as her primary language. As a result of this belief, the mother states she speaks to her daughter only in the English language.

> *"My daughter will be an American citizen. This is more important than her being a Hmong. I speak to my daughter in English. She will need to know English good. She will not need to know Hmong."*

The older Hmong participants that were interviewed for this study saw their children's ability to communicate in English as an advantage for the entire family. Younger Hmong participants were able to serve as the family's translators and negotiators for services and goods when their family was dealing with the outside world.

This older Hmong male shared that his children's ability to engage in English gave them a distinct advantage to understand and relate to the American community, something he felt that he was unable to do.

> *"I don't understand the Americans. I think that my children understand the Americans much more than I do. I just don't understand the American people."*

The younger Hmong participants that were interviewed expressed frustrations when attempting to communicate with the older Hmong, particularly parents and grandparents. Frequently, the interpretation of the young Hmong was not so much that their parents and grandparents were unable to communicate with them in English, but more so that their parents and grandparents did not understand how the American culture works.

This 14-year-old Hmong female described difficulties communicating with her mother. She felt her mother did not understand the younger Hmong generation, particularly the desire to be able to attend after school activities such as dances, games, and parties.

> *"My mother doesn't understand me. Like maybe when I learn something new from my friends or from my school and than I like want to do it or like I want to do other stuff, then my mother goes, 'like, you can't do that.' But all the other kids at school get to do it."*

The older Hmong participants frequently described a need to rely on their children to negotiate with the outside community. This reliance on the children to serve as translators and negotiators was based on the excelled ability of the children to converse in English. Further, the children had a deeper understanding than that of their parents of the nuances of the mainstream or dominant American culture.

This 50 year old female described her need to rely on her daughter to serve as a negotiator and translator when communicating with the non-Hmong speaking community.

> *"I try to learn English, but I don't learn it so good. I have a memory problem. Now, I have to ask my daughter to speak for me when I talk to the Americans. I don't know what else to do about it. My daughter, she knows more than I do about the American ways."*

Many of the older Hmong participants shared their concerns about their children wanting to be more like Americans and less like Hmong people. This transition within families created considerable tension among the older and younger Hmong.

The older Hmong participants believed that the American public school system provided a distinctive influence on their children. Further, the older Hmong participants felt that other American school-aged children were direct influences on their Hmong school-aged children. It was believed by many of the older Hmong participants that this influence from school and peers resulted in direct defiance of parental authority in the home.

In the traditional Hmong family, the father would have absolute authority. He would have the distinctive right to impose corporal punishment on disobedient children. However, all the Hmong participants interviewed understood only to well that corporal punishment was considered illegal in the United States of America.

The older Hmong participants perceived this protection of children from corporal punishment as disempowering for the parents, who would virtually have no control over the behavior of their children. Most of the older Hmong participants that were interviewed believed that their children had the authority to report them to the police department for being "bad" parents. These parents believed that their children could actually have them arrested and detained in jail for not being "good" parents.

This 50-year-old male shared his feelings of frustration as he perceived he had no power over his children when they did not listen to him.

> *"They don't listen to us anymore. We tell them*
> *and they don't care what we say. They are*
> *interested in their school and their friends.*
> *Even my daughters are considered equal to*
> *Their brothers in this country. They go to*
> *school with the boys, they are not separate.*
> *They are getting an education and can make up*
> *their own minds without me. In this country,*
> *children don't have to listen to the parents."*

The older Hmong participants lack of English speaking skills not only affected their ability to communicate with their non-Hmong speaking children, this also proved to be a challenge when negotiating within their work and their community. The older Hmong that were interviewed expressed considerable difficulty in communications with their employers and fellow co-workers.

As a result of the lack of communication with employers and co-workers, many of the older Hmong interviewed had expressed dissatisfaction at their workplace. Even the younger adult Hmong who were able to communicate relatively well and were comfortable speaking in English shared their secret fears of losing their jobs should they say anything at their work.

This 25-year-old Hmong male shared how he used to be afraid to talk to his supervisor before he began to understand the American culture.

> *"Before, I used to be scared of my boss. My boss would say something to me, and I would do whatever he would say to me. Then later, I learned from a friend at my work who is American, who understand the American ways. My friend said to me, that in this country, you do not have to be scared of your boss, nobody, not even the President of the United States. You can make him believe your way is right. After that, I don't ask nobody anymore. I know That I can make my own way because I am an American citizen now."*

Cultural and language barriers directly effect the understanding that these Hmong participants have about work and educational systems within the United States of America. Many of the older Hmong participants had never worked for an employer before moving to the United States. These older Hmong persons were farmers and businessmen in their home communities' back in Laos and Thailand.

Because of the small number of Hmong persons residing in Rochester, Minnesota, most of the adult Hmong participants that were interviewed worked in places where they were the only Hmong speaking people. Of those who were fortunate to work with other Hmong persons, they had little opportunity to speak with each other and usually only during their break times where they were able to communicate in their native language of Hmong.

This young male in his early twenties, speaks of the difficulties experienced by Hmong employees when adjusting to work life in the United States of America. He sees the language and cultural barriers faced at the work place by the Hmong people as the most difficult.

> *"Sometimes it is very difficult. There are no Hmong people at my work. So I always speak in English. There are a lot of Hmong working at my job, but we are all in different places. It is hard to let go of the*

> *past and it is hard to work here and make*
> *your way in this country. I wouldn't say*
> *letting go, but when we used to live in Thailand*
> *we were different than here. We had to change*
> *a lot of our ways and we had to learn English*
> *and how to live and work in America."*

The inability to effectively communicate in English with their employers was particularly complicated for the older Hmong participants. Frequently, the older Hmong interviewed had taken jobs that would be considered beneath them back in Laos or Thailand.

This fifty-year-old male shares deep feelings of frustration as he faces complex problems at his work place due to his lack of English speaking skills and his ability to share information with his supervisor and fellow co-workers.

> *"I don't know English so good. So when my boss*
> *talks to me, I know what he wants me to do, but*
> *sometimes I know a better way to do it. I want to*
> *tell him my way, but I don't have the words to tell*
> *him this. It makes my head just want to explode!*
> *I have so much in my head and I can't tell it to*
> *the other people around me."*

Communicating with the Rochester mainstream community and nearby neighbors has posed a particularly problematic situation for many of the older Hmong participants of this study. Limited English speaking skills, reliance upon their children and grandchildren to serve as negotiators and translators were found in eight out of the fifteen of the families interviewed.

This fifty-year-old female confided in the interview that she feels frustrated because she is unable to communicate with her neighbors and as a result she feels isolated within her community. She is unable to work because of a mental health disability. With her husband still missing in Laos, and her children gone all day to school and work, she is frequently left alone in a small apartment in a lower income neighborhood.

> *"I think this is a good neighborhood. But my*
> *only problem is I don't know my neighbors.*
> *I can't talk to them. No Hmong people live*
> *around here. The people that live here don't*

understand me and I don't understand them.
Before, there was one Hmong family that
lived here, but they moved away now to
Minneapolis. I think my neighbors are good
people, but I don't know for sure. I can't
talk to them and they can't talk to me."

The majority of the older Hmong participants shared a desire to communicate and establish a relationship with their non-Hmong speaking neighbors. Most of these older Hmong interviewed believed that they lived in good neighborhoods and shared an interest to be more active as a member within their neighborhood and community.

This 76-year-old Hmong male discussed his views about the neighborhood here he lives and his attempts to establish relationships without the ability to converse with his neighbors in the same language.

"We have good neighbors, I think. They smile to
me and wave to me when I walk by. They try to
talk to me and say hello. But I cannot speak to
them. All I can do is say hello back. I don't
speak in English. My son has to help me when
I speak to the neighbors. When I go for a walk
or a ride on my bicycle, people just smile and
wave to me. They are White people, no Hmongs
live around here. I wish that I could talk to
them. I think we could be good friends if we
could speak to each other. This is very difficult
for me."

The experiences of Hmong participants living in homogeneous neighborhoods of Rochester, Minnesota was not without conflict or differences. Three of the Hmong families interviewed for this study shared personal experiences of problems with one or more neighbors. These conflicts were frequently the result of a lack of understanding by the non-Hmong neighbor regarding the Hmong culture.

This 68-year-old male shared the problems he faced establishing a positive rapport and relationship with his non-Hmong neighbors. In particular, a problematic relationship with one White neighbor was not very easily resolved.

"I think one of our neighbors doesn't like us. He lives across the street and sometimes he shouts at us. I don't know what he is saying. But I see him giving me the finger, and I know what this means. I think he don't like that we have so many children. We don't want trouble but I know he doesn't like us. He is just like that. I am a United States citizen now, so I put my American flag outside my house. I hope he see that I am a respectful American now."

Education

The level of education of the Hmong participants was diverse and unique.   Formal education was directly linked to the age of each participating family member (Table 8.2).

Twenty-nine percent of the respondents had not received any type of formal education.   Eight percent of the participants had completed a baccalaureate degree at a four-year college and three of the participants (less than one percent) had received a two-year technical college degree.

Five of six respondents who had completed a formal education between grades first and sixth had done so while residing in the country of Laos. The remaining subjects who had received a formal education completed their studies while residing in the United States of America.

All the Hmong participants regardless of age or personal level of formal education considered achieving a higher education important.   Most of the younger adult Hmong who were married, believed that completing a formal high school education was necessary to obtain decent employment that would provide a livable wage.

The older Hmong participants expressed a desire to learn to speak English and to study reading and writing in English.   All the Hmong subjects reported that English as a Second Language (ESL) courses that were offered in Rochester, Minnesota were readily available to those who needed these courses.   Those Hmong participants enrolled in ESL classes believed they were adequate and worthwhile.

The number one reason cited by a Hmong participant for not attending ESL classes was having the time available to attend.   Second to this reason was Hmong participants who believed they were not learning English quickly enough.   These respondents did not hold the ESL classes or the

Table 8. 2 – Level of Formal Education

Family	Grades 1-6	Grades 7-11	High School	Technical	College
H01	1	2	1	0	0
H02	0	0	1	0	1
H03	0	2	0	0	0
H04	0	0	0	0	0
H05	0	2	0	1	0
H06	1	0	0	0	0
H07	0	1	1	0	0
H08	0	0	2	0	0
H09	0	0	0	0	1
H10	0	0	1	1	0
H11	0	0	0	1	1
H12	0	2	0	0	0
H13	2	1	0	0	0
H14	1	1	0	0	0
H15	1	0	0	0	0
TOTAL	6	11	6	3	3

ESL instructors responsible. These respondents believed their difficulties in learning the English language were the result of memory problems.

Employment

Employment and the difficulties of obtaining a job that provides a livable wage was of particular importance to the Hmong families that were participating in this study. Many of the older Hmong participants had no former history of working for an employer or an institution before arriving in the United States of America. Most of the older Hmong participants prior work history was in Laos and consisted mainly of farming and agricultural work.

Three of the older Hmong adults who participated in this study were Shaman, with one of these Hmong adults continuing to practice his trade in the United States. One of the older Hmong males was a carpenter in Laos and Thailand, but is employed in the United States in assembly line work.

Lack of prior work history and the inability to communicate in English has been a particularly challenging obstacle for all the older Hmong adults who have sought employment in the United States of America.

This fifty-year-old male describes some of the difficulties he has faced in finding and keeping suitable employment since residing in the United States.

> *"I worked for IBM, but I got laid off. I have to take a job as a janitor in a nursing home. I don't like my work, but I do not speak English so good. So I cannot find another job. In Laos, I have a nice and clean job as a nurse. I was trained by a doctor in Laos to be a nurse. I was good at this job because I was a Shaman and I am good at healing people. This is what I was made to do in this life. Now, in this country, I cannot be a nurse, I cannot be a Shaman, but I can be a janitor."*

Many of the Hmong participants of this study were working in factories or other blue-collar positions. The fear of losing one's employment was a prevalent theme in all those who were interviewed and working. A 34-year-old male who cares for his elderly mother and was the father of eleven children relied heavily on his income to support his large family. During the interview, he shared his decision to go back to school and earn a technical degree after the uncertainty of working in a factory in Iowa and being laid off.

> *"I been doing my own business since I moved to Rochester. I don't look for a job at all. When I was living in Des Moines, I worked for a beer factory, but I didn't like it. When they had a strike, I didn't go to work and then I had no money to feed my family. I hated this, because I had a job, but I was not allowed to work, because we are striking, so then I have no money. It was then that I decided to have my own business."*

There were a number of the Hmong families that relied on a female head of household as the main wage earner. Most of the older Hmong females interviewed had husbands that were considerably older. Several had husbands who were retired, or too old to find suitable work. Reliance on the income of a female head of household is a role reversal for most of the Hmong families. Traditionally, Hmong females are responsible for the care of the home, managing the household finances, and the keepers of Hmong culture and traditions.

With the lack of outside work skills and limited English speaking capabilities, the older Hmong women interviewed in this study that were working outside the home to contribute to the support of the family found jobs in assembly line work or in housekeeping. This 58-year-old mother shares feelings of job dissatisfaction and an inability to find suitable employment due to her lack of formal education and limited English speaking skills.

> *"I wish I could do better, I really don't like cleaning. I wish I was hired to do other work, but I don't speak in English so good. I don't read and I don't write, so I don't know how to fill out a job application. I think I have no chance in this life for a better job. I don't have any skills, but I know how to clean, so this is the job I must do."*

Traditional Hmong practices such as religion, played a key role in the lives of many of the Hmong persons interviewed. The belief in Animism and the concept of the spiritual world existing and living in all things, resulted in one older Hmong male's inability to find suitable employment in the United States. This 60-year-old male shared the unique problems he has faced as a practicing Shaman and how it has affected his ability to find suitable outside work that would not interfere with his responsibilities to the local Hmong community as a spiritual healer.

> *"One time I worked as a janitor. But I won't do this anymore because they make me use chemicals that smell bad and it make me to do my work as a Shaman, it messed up my spirits. The cleaning fluid spirits was working against my spirits and making it difficult for me as a Shaman. I had no choice, I had to leave this job. I am looking for another job, but I cannot find work. No one is looking for a Shaman or a teacher from Laos. No one will hire me to be a teacher, I have no education for a teacher and I don't see anyone saying that they are looking for a Shaman either."*

Lack of education was cited by several of the Hmong participants of this study as an impediment to locating suitable employment in the United States. This 50-year-old male was a carpenter in Laos and Thailand. He cites his lack of formal education in carpentry and his limited English speaking abilities as a barrier to his capability to receive a position in the work to which he is most familiar. He discusses the problems he has faced locating satisfactory employment.

> *"I work at a textile company and I fold clothes all day. I make very little money at this job. But we don't have time for education in our country. We were fighting for the American soldiers. We had no time for anything else. I used to be a carpenter when I lived in Laos and Thailand. I wish to work here as a carpenter, but I cannot pass the license test. When I go to see the carpenters working, I know what to do, but I don't know how to speak or write in English. In this country, everything is professional, everything is license. In my country, all you need is to know how to do it."*

The Welfare Reform and Social Responsibility Act of 1996 has resulted in many single, divorced, and widowed females having to seek employment or face the reduction or termination of their welfare benefits.

A 61-year-old divorced Hmong female who is the mother of ten currently receives welfare benefits from the state of Minnesota. She lives in a subsidized rental unit with her two minor children ages 9 and 14. She fears the termination of her welfare benefits because she is not currently looking for employment. Because of a physical and a mental disability, an inability to communicate in English, and lack of notable prior work experience, this single mother   fears the pressures received from her county eligibility worker to find a job.

> *My financial worker, she said to me that I need to go to work. But I never worked before in my life. I am 61 years old. The financial worker, she don't want to help me. She said to me, 'go to IBM, go apply to IBM.' But how do I get a job at IBM? I don't know how to get a job. Who will hire me? They want me to get a job, but no one will help me."*

Many of the Hmong families that participated in this study relied on the income generated from their teenage children. Income earned by each family member was to contribute to the survival of the entire family. Four of the eight Hmong teenagers interviewed were working part-time in such areas as fast food, grocery stores, and cashier positions. All eight of the teenagers that participated in this study were currently looking for employment.

This 18-year-old male was seeking part-time work after school and on weekends. He has hopes to one day go to college. He shares that he recognizes that he must contribute to the support of his family, and hopes that he can find a job with flexible work hours so he can continue with his education.

> *"I don't have much work experience. I have only worked for Taco Bell once . But I didn't like it very much. I want to get a job at the grocery store. But if I find any job at all, I'll take it."*

A 15-year-old Hmong female hopes to find work after school so she can help to support the rest of her family. She feels a great sense of responsibility to her family because there are fourteen people living in the home and her parents are not able to find work.

> *"I don't work right now, but I am looking for a job.*
> *My parents don't work so we need to help them by*
> *working. I am looking for a part-time job after my*
> *school and on weekends. "*

Another teenage Hmong is a 19-year-old and currently works part-time at a fast-food restaurant. Her father has been missing in action somewhere in Laos for a long time. Her mother is on disability for mental health reasons. She reports she is behind in her education and plans to graduate high school hopefully by next year. Her meager income helps the family to pay their utility bills and purchase groceries.

> *"I work part-time at Burger King when I am not in*
> *school. When we have summer vacation, then I will*
> *work even more. My mother is disabled and so she*
> *cannot work. My family needs the money I make.*
> *I help to pay for the electric bill and I buy the*
> *groceries. "*

Health Care

Twenty of the Hmong participants for this study (54 percent) reported having seen a medical doctor within the past four years. Visits to health care practitioners were based on the subject's current health and how he or she was feeling at the time. None of the Hmong subjects interviewed had seen a medical doctor for preventative care. All the Hmong participants interviewed only saw a medical doctor when they deemed it was necessary.

Most of the older adult Hmong subjects preferred to practice oriental medicine and frequently used herbal remedies for various ailments. Most of the older adult Hmong participants were reluctant to take allopathic medications either as an over-the-counter drug or as a prescription. ,

This 50-year-old male Hmong subject shared his experience taking an allopathic prescription medication. He related in the interview that the prescription medication made him feel drowsy and "not like" himself. Because of this, he discontinued the medication.

> *"I went to a doctor once. He gave me some medicine,*
> *but the medicine didn't help my problems. I stopped*
> *the medicine, because I don't' think this is good for*

you to take. I think the medicine in the United States
is useless."

A 50-year-old Hmong woman reported taking anti-depressants and anti-anxiety medications. She had been hospitalized twice for attempted suicides. She reported in her interview that she discontinued taking the anti-depressants and anti-anxiety medications given to her by her medical doctor after being released from the hospital the first time. The discontinuation of her medication resulted in a second mental breakdown and ultimately a re-hospitalization. She discontinued taking the medications a second time because she believed it was not helping her.

> *"I am okay. My problem is my health is not so good.*
> *I took medicine that the doctor gave me. But I don't*
> *take it anymore. I don't think this medicine helped*
> *me. The doctor put me in the hospital two times*
> *because I have too much stress. He gave me the*
> *medicine in the hospital . But I don't take it*
> *anymore after I came home. This medicine is no*
> *good."*

Of the 37 Hmong subjects that were interviewed, only two had been hospitalized for health problems since residing in Rochester, Minnesota. This 50-year-old Hmong male was hospitalized for acute appendicitis and he shared his experiences about the hospital and surgical procedures during the interview. He saw the medical system in the United States as being unresponsive to his need for medication to manage pain after the surgery.

> *"I had to go to the hospital for a surgery once. I had*
> *a pain in my side and the doctor gave me some*
> *medicine for it. Then the pain got worse and they*
> *had to do a surgery to take my appendix out. I was*
> *very sick and I had a lot of pain. But the doctor, he*
> *don't give me some medicine for the pain. I think,*
> *why don't American doctors give people medicine*
> *for pain? I just want the pain to go away, but the*
> *doctor, he don't help me."*

Fifteen of the thirty-seven Hmong subjects interviewed (41 percent) had seen a dentist in the past four years. Only one of the Hmong respondents, a 15-year-old female reported going for regular dental check-ups and cleanings every six months because of gum related problems. The remaining subjects in this study reported only going to the dentist when they believed it was absolutely necessary to do so.

A 19-year-old Hmong female reported during her interview that she was experiencing considerable pain in one of her teeth. She had seen a dentist recently. The dentist had informed her she had a cavity and would need a tooth filling. The subject did not return to the dentist to have this work done. She shared during the interview that she was afraid of the procedure as she had never had a tooth filling before.

> *"Well, I went to the dentist six months ago, because I have this sharp pain in my tooth. He said I need to have a filling, but I think this will hurt me more than the tooth hurts, so I won't go back."*

A 74-year-old Hmong participant of this study shared that she is unwilling to go to a dentist in the United States of America because she doesn't believe the dentists here are as good as the dentists in Thailand.

> *"I went to the dentist in 1992. I have dentures that they made for me in Thailand in 1984. I like them, these dentures are good. In 1992, the dentist in the United States made new dentures and I don't like them. I don't wear them, I still wear my dentures from Thailand. The dentist called me to come again, but I don't go. They don't make good dentures here, they don't feel good in my mouth."*

A significant number of the Hmong participants for this study did not go to the dentist because of lack of dental insurance and the inability to pay the expenses related to dental care. A 17-year-old male participant shared how he was willing to see a dentist when necessary, but his family could only afford emergency dental care.

> *"I went to the dentist one time when I had a pain in my mouth and I got a filling. But I don't have insurance to go to the dentist, so I don't go anymore. If I get another pain in my mouth, I will have to go again."*

Twenty-two of the Hmong participants for this study (59 percent) had reported never having seen a dentist in their lifetimes. All of the Hmong subjects who had not seen a dentist before reported having no reason to make such a visit. A 31-year-old male reported that he believes there was no reason to see a dentist when there is not a problem with your teeth. He shared his views during the interview on why he thinks Americans need to see a dentist regularly.

> *I never went to a dentist in my life. I don't have anything wrong with my teeth, so why would I go? I think the Hmong people usually have healthy teeth so most don't go to the dentist. Going to the dentist is a waste of money. Now, our younger children, they grew up here, and they eat too much sugar and are having more problems with their teeth. They will need to go to the dentists more."*

Eight of the thirty-seven Hmong respondents (22 percent) had been to an optometrist in the past four years. Ten of the respondents reported having had their eyes checked by the school nurse or that they had an eye examination from the Department of Motor Vehicles when they went for their driver's license. They equated these activities as having their vision examined.

A 15-year-old male reported having his eyes examined by the school nurse. The school had recommended to his family that he be considered for eyeglasses. His family was unable to pay the cost of the glasses, and so therefore he goes without.

> *"I need glasses, they checked out my eyes at school and said that I should get glasses. But we can't afford them, so I don't have any."*

A 60-year-old Hmong female reported during the interview that she has cataracts. Her medical doctor had recommended cataract surgery, but due to a lack of medical insurance coverage, the surgeon denied the request. She wears prescription eyeglasses, but reports during the interview that she is unable to see well, even with the eyeglasses. She is quite agreeable to having the cataract surgery whenever the surgeon will recommend the procedure.

"I have a film on my eyes and the doctor gave me glasses to wear. One doctor told me that I need surgery, but the other doctor says no. So I just have the eye glasses."

Several of the older adult Hmong participants had reported purchasing non-prescription eyeglasses at a drug or discount store. A 60-year-old male participant reported that he needed eyeglasses in order to read. He did not have vision care insurance and was unable to afford the cost of an eye examination and prescription eyeglasses.

"I need glasses to see good. But I just go to the store and buy the glasses. This is good enough for me."

Two of the thirty-seven Hmong participants for this study reported ever having gone to see a psychologist or other mental health professional. One Hmong respondent was a fifty-two-year old male and the other respondent was a fifty-year-old female. Both subjects reported suffering from a great deal of stress and depression. The fifty-two-year old Hmong male reported having served in the Laotian army during the Asian wars. He shares his experiences in the mental health system since becoming ill.

"When I first came to the United States, I got very sick. I had to see a psychologist and the doctor gave me a lot of medicines. I was very tired all of the time and I could not get out of my bed. I had no energy and my wife was very worried for me. The psychologist said to me that I had too much stress, it was so much stress that the doctor said I could not work. I had to get SSI. The psychologist didn't help me at all. He talked to me, but this is not a problem that is helped from talking. If I want to talk, I can talk to my family."

The fifty-year-old Hmong female participant reported suffering from horrid memories of the Asian wars and the grief she feels from her experiences and the fact that her husband is reportedly still missing in action somewhere in Laos.

"When I first come here to the United States, I was very worried. My husband is missing in Laos and I am here alone with my children. I would hear the noises of war, but I would be in my room here in the United States. I could not forget the war. My son is scared for me and he take me to the hospital. A psychiatrist say that I have depression and so much stress that I am a disabled person. They gave me medicine. So they disable me and give me SSI income."

Three of the thirty-seven Hmong participants reported having mental health related problems and seeking the help of a general medical practitioner. A fifty-year-old Hmong male described suffering from insomnia and an intense preoccupation with his past life in war-torn Laos.

"The doctor gave me some medicine once because I think so much about the past and then I can't sleep. I worry so much about the past. The medicine didn't help me. I didn't like to take it because I feel tired and then I can't work. So I stopped taking it."

A seventy-four-year old Hmong female expressed during her interview that she suffers from insomnia and hears voices. She expressed having internal conflicts as her past life in Laos as a Shaman interferes with her present life in the United States as a Christian Baptist.

"For a long time, I don't sleep because I hear the spirits of my ancestors calling to me. They are asking me why I leave my work as a Shaman? My ancestors asked me why I leave them. I asked them to go away because I live in the United States now and I am a Christian now. The ancestors are upset with me. The doctor gave me some medicine so that they don't talk to me anymore. The medicine did make them stop talking to me."

Another Hmong respondent, a sixty-one-year-old female, reported during her interview that she experiences regular and frequent occurrences of nightmares and feelings of being overwhelmed with her past and current life situation.

> *"My doctor helped me with my problems. He said to me that I am stressed and I am a very sad person inside. I have so many dreams of Laos and the Thai soldiers that killed a lot of Hmong people. The doctor gave me medicine to help me not feel so much stress. I don't like to take the medicine but I do it because I want to do what my doctor tells me."*

The majority of the Hmong participants that were interviewed for this study reported that they had no reason to see a mental health professional and saw their families as a means of emotional support and assistance in overcoming feelings of depression and stress. A twenty-five-year-old Hmong male reported during the interview that he doesn't know how talking to someone about his feelings will make his problems go away.

> *"Why would I go and talk to someone about my problems? Can they bring back my father? No, he is gone for good and there is nothing they can do to change this."*

Eight percent, or three of the thirty-seven Hmong participants reported currently taking prescription medications. Seven of the Hmong participants (19 percent) reported having to take a prescription medication at least one time in their lives. While twenty-seven of those interviewed (73 percent) had reported never taking a prescription medication in their lifetime.

Sixteen of the Hmong respondents (43 percent) had reported that they were currently taking or had taken herbal remedies to treat physical and mental health related problems. Two of the Hmong subjects reported taking daily prenatal vitamin supplements while pregnant, but have since discontinued. Twenty-eight of the thirty-seven Hmong participants (77 percent) that were interviewed reported having taken over the counter medications. All twenty-seven of these respondents cited Tylenol as an over the counter medication of choice for anything from headaches to flu to stomach ailments (Table 8.3).

The Hmong respondents varied in their responses on how they had learned about taking medications. The two Hmong females that had taken prenatal vitamin supplements while pregnant had reported that their obstetrician had prescribed the vitamins while they were pregnant.

The Hmong subjects who reported taking over the counter medications indicated they knew how to take medications such as Tylenol. They reported having learned this while in Thai refugee camps as it was a medication that readily available to them.

Older Hmong subjects who were unable to read or write in English reported asking a son or daughter for directions on how to take a prescription or over-the-counter medication. Those who were proficient in the English language responded during interviews that they would ask a doctor or pharmacist how to take a prescription or over-the-counter medication. A few of the Hmong respondents with higher comfort levels of English skills reported they would read the instructions on the bottle and then share the information with their non-English speaking family members.

The Hmong subjects who reported taking herbal remedies stated during the interviews that they received these medications from family members who were still in Laos or Thailand. The younger Hmong subjects that were taking herbal remedies noted they would ask an elderly Hmong how to take them as elder persons had more knowledge of herbal remedy usage.

Family Relationships

All of the Hmong participants for this study reported having positive and rewarding relationships with their families. However, each subject shared how family relationships have changed since moving to the United States.

Table 8.3 – Use of Medications						
Family	Age	Gender	Prescription	Herbal	OTC	Vitamins
H01	55	M	Y	Y	Y	N
	18	M	N	N	Y	N
	15	M	N	N	Y	N
	14	F	Y	N	Y	N
H02	25	M	N	Y	Y	N
	23	F	N	Y	Y	Y
H03	50	F	Y	N	N	N
	19	F	N	N	Y	N
	14	F	N	N	Y	N
H04	76	M	N	Y	N	N
	74	F	Y	Y	N	N
H05	34	M	N	N	Y	N
	17	M	N	N	Y	N
	15	F	N	N	Y	N
H06	68	M	N	Y	Y	N
	58	F	N	Y	Y	N
H07	60	M	N	Y	N	N
	53	F	N	Y	N	N
	21	M	N	Y	N	N
	15	F	N	Y	N	N
H08	21	M	N	N	Y	N
	19	F	N	N	Y	N
H09	31	M	N	Y	Y	N
H10	31	M	Y	N	Y	N
	30	F	Y	N	Y	N
H11	26	M	Y	N	Y	N
	23	F	N	N	Y	Y
H12	25	M	N	N	Y	N
	26	F	N	N	Y	N
H13	50	M	Y	Y	Y	N
	49	F	N	Y	Y	N
	15	F	N	N	Y	N
	13	F	N	N	Y	N
H14	61	F	Y	N	N	N
	14	M	N	N	N	N
H15	52	M	Y	Y	Y	N
	36	F	N	Y	Y	N

A twenty-five-year-old Hmong male saw his marriage to his wife as being more like an American husband and wife relationship more than a traditional Hmong marriage relationship. He points out that he believes his children will retain even less of the Hmong culture as they get older.

"I think that the elderly people have a different relationship than do younger people. My wife and I are more American and we are more equal. We don't share things like my mother and father do. I don't give my wife money like my father does to his wife. She has her own money. We are more American, but we still are Some Hmong too. Those Hmong younger than me, they will be less Hmong than me."

A 76-year-old Hmong male shared in his interview that he believes it is important for his children to retain some of the traditional Hmong values, but they should focus more on building a new life in the United States of America. He shares that is it important for a father to be a good role model for his children as it will ultimately pay off in that the children will in turn become better and more responsible adults and be positive role models for their own children.

"It doesn't matter what country you are living in. Just so long as you work hard and be a good role model to your children. If you do this, you will have good food to eat and a place to live. Your children will grow up and be good role models for their children. This is more important to me than if my children are more American or more Hmong. I want them to work hard and to be good people."

Many of the older adult Hmong expressed how their relationships with their children was different than the types of interactions parents have with their children in Laos. The changes in parent and child relationships that have occurred for these Hmong families has created some conflicts as the parents have attempted to gain control over their relationships with their children.

The younger Hmong adults expressed similar concerns over their relationships with parents. These younger Hmong adults believed that their parents did not understand how life in the United States was for young adults or teenagers. They perceived the parents' interventions as unreasonable or unnecessary.

This 34-year-old Hmong male shared his attempts at trying to gain control in his home where his children have been influenced by American cultural perceptions that are different from their Hmong parents.

> *"My children have a different culture from me and my wife. They are more American. They think they can do whatever they want to do. I tell them all the time, if they want to be like an American person, they should pay me rent to live here in my house. They should pay for their own food, like American parents do to their children. Otherwise, I tell them, if you live in my house, you live by my rule. I say, if they want their own rule, they should move out or pay me rent."*

Many of the young and married adult Hmong saw significant changes in their own children to a more American lifestyle as being a positive occurrence. These younger married adult Hmong pointed out that life in the United States of America is an improvement from Laos. Education and job opportunities were cited the most frequently as a chance for their children to have a better life.

A 31-year-old Hmong male reported during the interview that his children's adaptation to the American lifestyle is positive.

> *"Oh, I think things have changed since we are here. I think my kids have a much better life here than I had in Laos and Thailand. Over here the government and laws are more organized. Education is available for everyone here and is easy to get. We tell our children that life is good here. I think for the older people, it is hard to live in this country, because they don't speak English, but the younger people, they are happy here and like living here."*

Community Integration

Integration into the community for the Rochester area Hmong was comprised of several different components: 1)   Understanding the American Legal System;   2)   Banking and Credit;   3)   Driving and Transportation and;   4)   Shopping.

Twenty-seven of the Hmong respondents (73 percent) reported they had little or no understanding of the American legal system. The ten respondents (27 percent) who reporting having some knowledge of the American legal system and how it works shared that they learned about this while in an American High School.

Older Hmong respondents reported that they had no knowledge of how the American legal system works. They believed that this information was not important as it did not apply to them personally. A 76-year-old Hmong male shared his thoughts that as long as a person doesn't get into any trouble with the law, then there is no need to know about how the legal system works in America.

> *"I don't know anything about this. Maybe my son knows. I do know that you should obey the police and you won't get into any trouble."*

A 34-year-old married, Hmong male respondent shared his belief that information about the American legal system is made known to people if and when they are experiencing problems with the law.

> *"I don't know a whole lot about this. I do know that if you get into trouble that you have to go to court and tell the judge. If you tell the judge the truth, then he will help you."*

The above respondent's 15-year-old daughter disagrees with her father's views. She believes that it is important for a person to know about how the American legal system works. She shares that she is learning how the legal system in America works in her classes at high school.

> *"We learned about this in school and stuff. How the United States government works and stuff like that. You read about that stuff in school. Like you talk about it in political science class and stuff."*

Eleven of the thirty-seven Hmong subjects (30 percent) reported having a checking or savings account in a United States bank. Of the twenty-six respondents who did not have a checking or savings account, ten (27 percent) were aged 13 to 19 years. Five of the older Hmong participants (14 percent) interviewed reported having a son whom managed their finances for them. These same five subjects reported their sons as the responsible person for handling the family budget and paying the bills.

Ten of the subjects interviewed (27 percent) reported having a credit card. All of the Hmong participants who possessed credit cards reported using them for emergency purposes only and then paying off the entire amount when the bill came due. Several of the participants reported not having interest in possessing a credit card as they believed that this only encouraged people to buy what they could not afford.

Eight of the Hmong interviewed (22 percent) reported having a small savings account. The remaining twenty-nine participants shared similar concerns about an inability to save due to a lack of available financial resources. Three of the Hmong participants (8 percent) had small investments in retirement accounts, CDs, money market accounts, or mutual funds.

Seventeen of the participants (46 percent) possessed a valid Minnesota driver's license. Four of these Hmong subjects reported having received a speeding ticket in the past four years. None of the Hmong participants reported ever having an automobile accident. Of those respondents who were of legal age to drive but did not have a license, the majority reported the reason as being an inability to pass the written driver's examination because of a lack of ability to read and write in English.

Fourteen of the fifteen Hmong families that participated in this research owned an automobile. All fourteen families reported carrying automobile insurance and understood that carrying insurance on one's automobile was required by the state of Minnesota. The one family that did not own an automobile reported relying on public transportation when venturing out in the community.

All thirty-seven of the Hmong interviewed had reported that access to shopping was easily attained. There are six Asian grocery stores in Rochester, Minnesota and all the subjects reported an ability to find the types of foods preferred for a Hmong diet. All respondents reported eating Hmong foods a majority of the time and that they believed this type of diet to be healthy.

Eight of the respondents (22 percent) reported knowledge of how to cook some American-style foods. The American-style foods most often prepared by the Hmong participants were: spaghetti, pizza, hot dogs, and hamburgers. All thirty-seven Hmong participants reported eating American-style foods at least occasionally. The most commonly cited American-style food consumed was take-out pizza.

All of the families interviewed had reported having at least one person in the household that knew how to operate kitchen appliances, washing machines, clothes dryers, and other home appliances.

Chapter 9

Analysis of Cultural Awareness

One of the most important components in the transmission of culture is language (Barresi, 1987.) Language affects and reflects a person's thoughts, feelings, and actions. Language is used by human beings to interpret their environment and the world that surrounds them.

Intergenerational differences of parents and children from migrant and refugee families resulting from barriers in the language spoken are well documented in the literature.

Osako (1979) reported language barriers between Japanese born parents and their American born children. These barriers often prohibited the sharing of crucial and intimate family information between parents and children. Osako also noted that American born children would often find it difficult to express information of a delicate nature to their Japanese born parents.

Kendis (1989) reported that first generation parents would often listen to and later ask someone to translate what was said between their second-generation children and their third generation grandchildren. According to one participant in Kendis's study: *"When my children and grandchildren talk, it is in English. I understand a little bit but I have to go aside with someone afterwards to get a translation of what has been said. Sometimes, I think I was following the conversation, understanding some of the words, but I find out I was completely wrong in my interpretation."*

The older Hmong adults (30 percent of the participants) interviewed for this research reported having difficulties communicating with their children. This was highlighted most significantly from the differences in languages spoken, the interpretations of Hmong and American cultures, and the ability to control the nature of the relationship between parents and children.

The younger adult Hmong (38 percent of the participants) from this study believed that it was important for families to retain some of the Hmong culture and values, but also to be able to embrace the American culture and way of life. The younger adult Hmong would lean more toward the American culture and way of life as they deemed it necessary for survival in the society to which they are currently residing. These younger adult Hmong perceived the Hmong culture as an important part of their history and heritage, but not as a necessary component for survival in the United States of America.

The pre-adult Hmong (32 percent of the participants) that were interviewed believed it was more important to learn about the American culture and let go of the older Hmong traditions and beliefs. These pre-adult Hmong participants viewed the Hmong culture as irrelevant to their survival within the United States of America. Problems in communication and misunderstandings occurred between pre-adult Hmong and older Hmong because of the differences in the comfort levels in the English and Hmong languages.

Although these findings of describing the hardships that occur in immigrant and refugee families due to language barriers and differences is not new, a study that discusses the ramifications of language barriers on intergenerational connectedness and feelings between the generations is relatively new to cultural studies.

Von Hassel (1993), found through interviews with first generation parents and their second-generation children that adult children held vague impressions about their parents' lives. Von Hassell surmised that culture and societal pressures, coupled with the waning of the native language within the household and the lack of emphasis on the culture of origin acted as a silence barrier for first generation parents. The second-generation children have very little information about their parents' background or prior life experiences, because the parents spoke in a different language or did not communicate in the same manner as the children.

The differences in understanding and information about each others cultures was noted in the interviews with the older adult, younger adult, and pre-adult Hmong that participated in this study. Most of the younger adult Hmong and all of the pre-adult Hmong cited a higher comfort level speaking in English.

Older adult Hmong family members reported having a higher comfort level speaking in Hmong with limited English speaking ability. Some of the pre-adult Hmong family members reported having very limited ability to speak in Hmong. These pre-adult Hmong frequently relied on their older siblings to serve as translators for them when speaking with the parents. This was particularly crucial when the communication was related to very delicate or complex interactions.

Blocked communication resulting from the ability to engage in each other's language between the generations of a family undoubtedly results in the disintegration of shared experiences as well as the understanding of one and other within the generations. Further, blocked communication can significantly heighten the levels of stress within the family environment.

Von Hassel (1993) asserted that first generation parents would strive to reduce such tension resulting from blocked communication by presenting an acceptance of their second generation children becoming more American and not wanting to hinder their children's success within the United States.

This attempt at the reduction of tension was noted when the older adult Hmong participants would share how it was more important that their children were good people who studied or worked hard. These older adult Hmong shared the belief that it was less important what their children understood or knew about Laos and being a Hmong person.

Within this study, when the older adult Hmong were asked what it means to be a Hmong person in the United States of America, they listed cultural practices and values that they hoped their younger generations would pass on to their children. The most frequently cited practices and values that the older adult Hmong hoped to be retained were language, commitment to family and clan, the celebration of the Hmong New Year, a sense of self-awareness as a Hmong person, traditional Hmong art, crafts, songs, and dances.

When the younger adult Hmong were asked what it means to be a Hmong person residing in the United States of America, they were more likely to struggle in their search for a response.

These younger adult Hmong have come to the realization that their generation will have to carry the responsibility for defining the Hmong culture within the United States of America for their children and future generations. Many of these younger adult Hmong were concerned that they did not have a sufficient understanding of the Hmong culture and traditions necessary to pass on these ideals to their children and to future generations of Hmong residing in the United States of America.

REFERENCES

Barresi, C.M., (1987). Ethnic Aging and the Life Course. In D.E. Gelfand and C.M. Barresi (Eds.). *Ethnic Dimensions of Aging.* New York City, NY: Springer Publishing Company.

Kendis, R.J., (1989). *An Attitude of Gratitude: The Adaptation to Aging of the Elderly Japanese in America.* New York City, NY: AMS Press.

Osako, M., (1979). Aging and Family Among Japanese Americans. The Roles of Ethnic Tradition in the Adjustment to Old Age. *The Gerontologist.* 19: pp. 448-455.

Von Hassel, M., (1993). Issei Women: Silence and Fields of Power. *Gender Studies.* 19: pp. 549-569.

Chapter 10

Theme Two – Ethnic Loyalty

All of the Hmong persons that were interviewed for this research project reported the first language they learned to speak was Hmong. Twenty-one of the thirty-seven participants (57 percent) reported the language they were most comfortable speaking was in Hmong. Eighteen of the thirty-seven subjects interviewed (49 percent) could read in Hmong. Fifteen of the thirty-seven participants interviewed (41 percent) could write in Hmong.

The written form of the Hmong language is very recent in modern history. The Hmong language was not available in the written format until sometime in the 1950's. Formal education for the majority of older adult Hmong was virtually non-existent while residing in Laos. Most of the eighteen Hmong participants who were able to read and write in Hmong were older adult males.

The average number of years in formal education for older adult Hmong that went to school in Laos was three years or the equivalent of third grade in the United States of America. This 50-year-old Hmong female shared during her interview that Hmong girls did not normally go to school in Laos, but instead learned how to care for house and family by their elder females.

> "I only speak good in Hmong, but when I was a little girl, I also learned to speak in Laos. I don't read or write because I don't have an education when I was a young girl, they don't send girls to school in Laos. I don't know any read or write. I never go to school so I could learn these things, I only work to help my parents on our farm, then

when I was old enough, I got married."

Many of the Hmong participants that were interviewed for this study lived in remote villages and rural areas of Laos prior to moving to the United States of America.   In these remote places of Laos, formal education and public schooling was not readily available. Those who were able to receive some type of formal education prior to life in the United States of America were living in larger cities and urban areas of Laos.

This 21-year-old Hmong male shared during the interview process that his family lived in a remote village in the mountainous region of Laos. There were no schools available for the residents. As with many of the Hmong participants that were interviewed in his age group, his family fled Laos when he was quite young. Once situated in a refugee camp in Thailand, he was able to attend school for the first time. However, his education was in the Thai language and not in Hmong.

> *"When I was young, I was speaking in Hmong. I know how to speak it very well. But we don't have a school in Laos for me to go, so I never went to school in Laos. When I was a young boy, we moved to Thailand and they don't teach us in Hmong there. Because of this, I don't read and write in Hmong."*

None of the pre-adult Hmong participants that were interviewed for this research were able to read and write in the Hmong language.   The opportunity to learn reading and writing in Hmong is not readily available in the United States of America for the younger Hmong generations. Many of these pre-adult Hmong were not interested in learning to read and write in the Hmong language. As this 15-year-old Hmong male shares in the interview, he is not interested in learning to read and write in his native language and deems it much more important to become proficient in reading and writing of the English language.

> *"I don't care much about it really. I don't know how to read and write in that language and I don't really want to learn it. There is no point because I live here now and it is more important to know the English language."*

Two of the Hmong participants of this study who were able to read and write in the Hmong language were self-taught. This 49-year-old Hmong female never received a formal education, but shares that she taught herself to read and write in the Hmong language.

> *"I teach myself to read and write in Hmong. I*
> *never go to school in my entire life. I read and*
> *write a little bit, so this is the best that I can do.*
> *Because I never go to school in my life time, I*
> *know just a little bit. I can't read and write*
> *in English even a little bit."*

Traditions and Rituals

In the research process, the topics of ethnic loyalty were intertwined with cultural awareness. Ethnic loyalty refers to the Hmong participant's desires to retain a sense of Hmong identity while at the same time, cultural awareness refers to the Hmong participants willingness to learn about American values, beliefs, and customs.

The range of ways that a Hmong refugee could show their Hmong identity after establishing residence in the United States of America is limited. In the country of Laos, the Hmong language, home life, work as farmers in the mountains and as entrepreneurs of their country, specific rituals during the Hmong New Year, particular treatment of the deceased members of the clan, dressing according to one's tribe, political loyalty to one's own clan, and certain assumptions about social hierarchy within the clan and the household provide the backbone of what is meant by being a Hmong person.

The importance of the Hmong New Year to the participants of this study cannot be overstated. Each year in December, some 400 Hmong persons come together at the Olmsted County fairgrounds to attend a New Year celebration. The event lasts for twelve hours and offers the participant's food, drink, music, dancing, native costumes, speeches and presentations from clan elders. All of the fifteen Hmong families that were interviewed for this research discussed the significance of the New Year to their identity as a Hmong person. The Hmong New Year is the only formal holiday celebrated and recognized by the Hmong people.

The Hmong families that participated in this research believed the New Year event was the most meaningful way to provide their children an opportunity to experience the Hmong culture first hand.

*The Hmong New Year Celebration is an opportunity
for friends, both old and new to get together.*

As a 25-year-old Hmong male and father of two, this participant shares how the Hmong New Year is one of the most significant ways that he can share the Hmong culture with his children.

> *"We have to go every Hmong New Year. It is so important to us and it is only once a year. The Hmong New Year shows us that we are who we are and that we should be proud of being Hmong. We also show the young people that they are Hmong people too, not just American people. That is the only most important thing we can do to keep our culture alive . So people will understand we are Hmong first, American second."*

A 74-year-old Hmong woman discusses her belief that the Hmong New Year is a way of passing down the traditions from one generation to another, allowing for younger children to understand their Hmong heritage and culture of origin. She believes, along with many of the Hmong, that without this holiday, the younger generations would not be able to truly appreciate their heritage.

> *"The Hmong New Year is very important to us. Generations will pass to new generations who we are. We do not want to lose one generation by not doing this. This is why it is so important to do every year. The young learn about our people and our culture and what we had as a people before we came here."*

A number of the pre-adult Hmong that were born in the United States of America are not as enthusiastic as the older generations about attending the Hmong New Year celebration. A 26-year-old married Hmong male with children fears that the younger generations do not have an interest in attending the Hmong New Year celebration in Rochester. He believes that over time, this important Hmong holiday will fade away and the Hmong culture, heritage, and traditions will pass away with it.

> *"I think the Hmong New Year is very important and the children can learn about the Hmong culture this way. But I think the young children are not so interested, and their children will be*

> *less interested. I am afraid they will not want*
> *to know about the Hmong ways. Then they will*
> *be Americans all of the time. They won't want*
> *to know about Hmong ways and it will be lost*
> *over time."*

Hmong families are traditionally patriarchal and organized by group or clan. These traditional family roles have remained stable throughout many centuries of Hmong people. Historically, men have held the leadership roles for both home and community, as well as having the primary responsibility of raising sons.

Sons, particularly the eldest son have carried the responsibility as the head of household in the case of the father's instability or absence. Women have predominantly been responsible for childbirth, tending to the homes, assisting in the fields, and teaching the Hmong traditions to their children.

The Hmong families interviewed for this research have had to make some accommodations in the way family matters are handled since moving to the United States of America. This is in large part due to the younger Hmong exposures to the United States educational and social institutional systems. Despite this need for accommodation, many family roles have remained intact for these Hmong.

A 25-year-old married Hmong male believes that the eldest son has the responsibility to care for the parents in their old age. He shares his views on the elder son's responsibility and obligation to family and parents.

> *I think it is important for me to live near to my*
> *parents. This is because my parents are getting*
> *older and they need me more. I believe that we*
> *must take care of our elderly people. One day,*
> *when they are older and can't take care of*
> *themselves , they will come to live with me and*
> *my family, so that I can take care of them.*
> *That is why we have children, that is what we*
> *the Hmong people believe. Having children is*
> *for helping when you get older, that is what*
> *believe, what we believe."*

An interesting change to the Hmong patriarchal traditions since moving to the United States of America, has been the responsibilities of Hmong children in serving as cultural brokers and translators for their older parents. This 26-year-old Hmong male goes on to share how his role, as the oldest son of the family has changed to that of leader in negotiations with mainstream American culture. In effect, on matters related to the United States culture and community, his father, a clan elder himself, defers to his son for advice.

> *"I think the oldest son should be responsible for all his family. In the Hmong culture, the oldest son has this responsibility. Right now, in this U.S. culture, I make decisions about American matters and my father makes decisions about Hmong matters. I think this works out good for us, because I know more about the U.S. things and my father knows more about the Hmong things."*

Overwhelmingly, the older adult Hmong participants that were interviewed for this study believed that their younger adult children, particularly the male children, should live close to their parents and family and provide elders with support in their old age. In Laos, there would be no question of the responsibility of sons to live with and care for the older adult Hmongs. However, the older adult Hmongs interviewed indicated they would be supportive of an adult child's desire, even the eldest son, to move if it was related to job prospects that would clearly benefit the family.

This 74-year-old Hmong female believes that adult children should live near their parents, but recognizes that this may not always be possible in the United States.

> *"The oldest son should help his parents and his family. He should live as close as possible to his parents. But the problem is, in this country, a person must live where he can work. If the son has to work somewhere that is far from the parents, he will need to do this so the family can survive. A son should not just go because he wants to move away. He should think of what is best for his whole family and make the decision of what is best to do."*

Teaching the young children in Hmong families about the culture was expressed by all the older and younger adult Hmong interviewed as important. However, all the Hmong families that were interviewed recognized that their children may not be interested in following or practicing traditional Hmong culture. A 22-year-old married female with children states she spends her time teaching her children about the Hmong history and way of life, but believes that they will be heavily influenced by the American culture, particularly once they are old enough to attend school.

> *"We try to tell our children more about the Hmong culture, but I think they will become more like American anyway and they will learn to do more this way. I think my children will be more like American. Maybe it will make problems and maybe it will not. I don't know for sure. I worry that their will is too strong and they will do what they want to do. They don't like to listen to me sometimes. They don't like sometimes even to listen to their father. We have to work more hard to get them to listen than our parents did for us."*

The Hmong social structure promotes family and the clan. A patriarchal system determines the clan fellowship, in which women once married, become members of the husband's family. All members within the same clan, or with the same last name, even when there is no blood relationship, are encouraged to intermarry their children so that the "blood will stay in the family." Therefore, marriage between first and second-degree cousins is relatively common.

With only thirty-eight Hmong families residing in Rochester, Minnesota, there are few available marriage options for the families with growing children. Most of the younger adult Hmong interviewed for this study who were married had to search for a spouse outside of the city of Rochester.

The pre-adult Hmong that were interviewed expressed a desire to date and ultimately make their own decision about locating, selecting, and eventually marrying a mate. This 53-year-old Hmong female shares her concerns that the Hmong culture will be lost to her children, particularly when she and her husband are no longer around to share it.

"If my husband pass away and I pass away, all the old people, from the old country, we all pass away, then our Hmong culture will be lost. My son's generation and my grandson's generation will no longer know about our Hmong culture and history. Our culture and our history will pass away, just like we the people will pass away."

Chapter 11

Analysis of Ethnic Loyalty

Cultural traditions and ethnic identification are important components of a person's individual and family identity. This family and personal identity emerge regardless of whether it is in actual behaviors, attitudes, or feelings.

The older adult Hmong participants that were interviewed for this study held strong to their ethnic identification and cultural heritage and traditions. These traditions held a powerful influence on expectations held of other family members, persons that were involved with the family decision making processes, and the development of the shared meanings of experiences as it related to life in the United States of America.

The older adult Hmong participants that were interviewed desired to raise their children as Hmong and teach their children about the Hmong history, traditions, heritage, culture, and celebrations. These older adult Hmong expressed through the interviews the importance held on family, tradition, respect for elders, and the responsibilities of children, especially the oldest son, to the parents.

The younger adult Hmong participants that were married and raising families of their own recognized the importance of traditions, heritage, culture, and celebrations, but knew very little about the history of the Hmong people and deferred to their elder family members on this subject. These young adult married Hmong subjects stressed the importance of family, respect for one's elders, and responsibilities of adult children, particularly the oldest son, in caring for elder family members. However, the younger adult Hmong believed that their own children would become more Americanized over time and that the Hmong culture and traditions would be lost to them.

The pre-adult Hmong participants that were interviewed for this study placed less importance on the Hmong traditions and celebrations. They knew very little about the history of the Hmong people and did not believe that this was important knowledge for them to acquire.

The pre-adult Hmong did believe that family was important and that one should respect elders and parents. However, the majority of the pre-adult Hmong participants questioned the roles and responsibilities of adult children to their parents. This was especially noted by pre-adult Hmong in relation to gender and the importance placed on the eldest son.

Of particular interest were the responses from the seven Hmong pre-adult female participants that were interviewed. These pre-adult Hmong female subjects questioned the authority that was granted to their male siblings and shared experiences where they directly disobeyed the requests of an older brother. Most of the pre-adult Hmong subjects believed that gender should have less importance within the family hierarchy and that age should carry more weight in the ability of one sibling to serve as an authority figure over another sibling.

Ethnic identification is so fundamental to family life that it actually colors all the important issues faced by immigrant and refugee families. Issues such as marriage, death, care of family members, health care, education, and employment are all directly influenced by an immigrant or refugee family's sense of cultural tradition and ethnic identification.

The older adult Hmong participants that were interviewed for this study stressed the importance placed on elders. The older family and clan members are responsible for making all decisions that are considered to be in the best interests of the children and the family as a whole.

The issue of selection of an eligible marriage partner for an adult Hmong child was considered to be a decision best left to the parents, particularly the father. The older adult Hmong subjects believed that it should be the father who would serve as ultimate decision maker for all matters that directly influence the family unit.

Further, the older adult Hmong participants believed that the mother should be responsible for sharing and passing down of Hmong traditions, keeping family members involved in heritage and history of the Hmong, and developing a sense of appreciation for Hmong culture in the children.

It should be noted that the majority of the Hmong families that were interviewed for this research had selected one family member, generally a younger adult or teenager, to serve as the family cultural broker, negotiator and translator when interacting with the mainstream society of Rochester.

The responsibilities placed upon these younger adult or teenage Hmong family members created a significant change within the balance and power structure of the Hmong families that were interviewed. This change was unique and quite different from the traditional Hmong family structure that was found by these subjects when residents of Laos and Thailand.

Ethnic identification and cultural history often supply a sense of continuity and meaning for older adult Hmong who are frequently bombarded with one demand after another to adapt to an ever changing and technologically driven American society.

The second and third generations of Hmong persons tend to differ from their elder counterparts as they seek out ways to alter the family traditions in varied degrees as a way of coping and adapting to the demands of the host society and mainstream culture.

As a result, it is not surprising to note intergenerational conflicts and gaps that arise within the Hmong families of this study. The modifications in family and cultural traditions by the children and grandchildren have certainly been a challenge for the older adult family members. Many of the older adult Hmong struggle in their attempts to understand their children as they become increasingly more American.

The older adult Hmong do recognize that their children and grandchildren will naturally become more Americanized, but acceptance to this fact is limited and more along the lines of resignation to the fact that this will occur whether they chose it or not.

The younger married adult Hmong participants have been able to find a more middle ground, or compromise between the two cultures – Hmong and American – and have expressed a greater acceptance of their children's desire to become more American.

The pre-adult Hmong that were interviewed for this study shared their frustrations from the lack of understanding of the two cultures – Hmong and American. These pre-adult Hmong subjects believed that it was more important to their survival in the United States to become more like Americans and did not see the significance or importance on the Hmong culture or its traditions.

Chapter 12

Theme Three – Migration Experience

According to the Diagnostic and Statistical Manual of Mental Disorders, 4th Edition (DSM-IV, 1994), persons who have emigrated from areas of considerable social unrest and conflict can experience elevated levels of Post Traumatic Stress Disorder.   Such persons may be particularly reluctant to discuss their experiences of trauma due to their sense of vulnerability as residents of a new host country.

The Hmong people have faced many hardships before arriving in the United States of America. Many Hmong persons have painful memories of the Asian Wars and their own often traumatic journey from Laos to Thailand.   Twenty-three of the thirty-seven Hmong subjects for this research (62 percent) expressed having vivid, extensive, and painful memories of the wars and their family's personal journey from Laos to Thailand. The remaining fourteen Hmong participants (38 percent) were either to young to remember or were not born until after their family arrived in Thailand or in the United States of America.

Several of the older adult Hmong that were interviewed suffer from a medically diagnosed condition of depression or post-traumatic stress disorder. This older adult Hmong female shared her experiences of post-traumatic stress and ultimately a major depressive episode that resulted in her being hospitalized twice in the past three years. Her persistent mental illness and resulting hospitalizations could be directly linked to her memories of living in a war torn country and of a husband who is still considered missing in action somewhere in the country of Laos.

"I had to go to the hospital because I am crying too much. My husband is CIA and he is missing in Laos. I still hear noises from the war. I remember Things and it is hard for me...I cannot forget it. The doctor say to me that I have stress and depression. They tell me that I have a medical breakdown. Because I remember Laos and I remember the Hmong people. So, I have to go to the hospital. They say I cannot work and that I am disabled. They give me SSI now."

The older adult Hmong participants emphasized the life experience differences between the United States of America and Laos throughout the interview process. An overarching theme was the anxiety that was faced by all of the Hmong subjects from a lack of financial resources since moving to the United States. Most of the Hmong participants excessively worried about paying bills and making ends meet.

An older adult female Hmong shared her feelings of frustration about living in a society where bills come faster and are greater than one's monthly income. This was intertwined with her desire to return to her homeland of Laos. Not the Laos of the present time, but the Laos of her past. The realization that she may never be able to return to the Laos she remembered, only intensified her feelings as she described not having the financial resources to meet her physical and emotional needs.

"I have too many worries in this country. I worry about money and paying bills. I really feel homesick and I miss Laos. The outside doesn't look like home and the inside doesn't look like home to me. In this country, we have food and clothing, we have a shelter, but my insides are broken to pieces. I wish I could go home one day, but I don't know if this will be possible."

An older adult Hmong male shares his experiences from untreated post traumatic stress disorder. He reports having frequent and reoccurring memories that are terrifying and intrusive. These recollections revolve around his involvement in the Asian Wars. He shared during the interview, that he is unable to watch movies about war because of the array of unpleasant memories that will ensue as a result. He reports he feels frequently restless and on edge. He shares that sudden noises remind him of certain events that occurred while he served in the military.

> *"Yeah, I remember the fighting. Sometimes, you are just sitting and doing nothing and it just all comes back to you. Sometimes, in my own house, if I hear a loud noise, I think it is a grenade or gunfire. I can't watch movies about the war, it is too hard. I like to see them, but they are too hard for me to watch. Because you watch and you know that some people are going to get hurt."*

Post traumatic stress disorder can occur at any age, even in young children. Those Hmong participants who were interviewed that had recollections of their family's journey from Laos to Thailand, overwhelmingly expressed experiencing feelings of intense fear and helplessness. Most of the younger adult Hmong participants shared how they were wakened in the middle of the night by their parents and told that the family had to leave right away. These younger Hmong became suddenly uprooted from the life that they once knew.

These young adult Hmong shared experiences of loved ones disappearing or watching as a loved one died. These painful experiences continue to haunt these younger adult Hmong years later.

This younger adult Hmong male recalls fleeing Laos as a young boy and of the journey with his family to Thailand. Like many of the younger adult Hmong participants who had memories of this journey, the deep sense of dread and anxiety is expressed for an unknown enemy known only as "them". The memory comes from the eyes of children, who have heard from parents that "they" will kill us if "they" find us. These memories come back to the younger adult Hmong repeatedly. For this particular male, the experiences are renewed in frequent nightmares that wake him in the middle of the night, leaving him unable to return to sleep.

> *"I remember when we left Laos for Thailand and there was some fights going on. We had to hide a lot during the day and I was very scared. I remember thinking that maybe we don't make it to Thailand, maybe they find us and kill us. I don't think you ever forget this feeling. I have dreams about it. Sometimes even when*

*I am awake and I think about it, it scares me
all over again. I try hard to get it from my
mind. I try to tell myself that it is past and
gone and now I have a future in this country."*

This 61-year-old Hmong female has become estranged from her husband since moving to the United States. Post traumatic stress disorder can severely affect marital and family relationships as it has for this female with children. This older adult Hmong female relates how her memories of the war were crippling and have affected her abilities to adjust and function to a new life in the United States of America. It is interesting to note that in her vivid description of a nightmare she has frequently, the Thai soldiers kill her estranged husband, yet she somehow manages to survive brutal beatings.

*"Every night I go to bed, I have the same dream
where I see dead Hmong people and soldiers
coming. I am hiding in the dream and it wakes
me up. No one knows how horrible this is for
me. I dream that I try to escape Laos and I get
caught by the Thai soldiers. The Thai kill my
husband and beat me so badly that I am mostly
dead. I see Hmong crossing the Mekong River
and I see Thai soldiers come and steal
everything they have and kill them. The
Mekong River is filled with the blood of the
Hmong people by the hands of the Thai soldiers."*

Refugee Experience

In the United States of America, many of the Hmong live in urban settings, dress like Americans, and make their livings however they can in the current available job market. There has been an upheaval in clan politics and loyalty as the Hmong strive for effective leadership within a new country and a new and alien political system.

Often a barrier, more than an opportunity, English is the language of formal education, rituals are diluted and stifled because of communities that do not embrace the Hmong culture, and more Hmong have conformed to Christianity in an attempt to fit into a society they know little about.

Based on these cultural changes, what then remains as the cornerstone of Hmong identity? For many families it is wearing Hmong clothing on special occasions such as the Hmong New Year, weddings, and funerals. It is also the ability to speak in their native language at home, and maintaining some semblance of a traditional family structure in the home.

This fourteen-year-old Hmong female was born in Thailand and spent of majority of her childhood life in the United States of America. She has never been to the country of Laos and knows very little about it. In her personal interview for this study, she described her perceptions of how American and Hmong cultures are different, with a personal preference for the American culture. This pre-adult Hmong female shared with the interviewer that she has a great interest in reading teen romance novels, resulting in her dreams of eventually finding a mate of her own and falling in love. This view is in direct conflict with the Hmong tradition of having the parents arrange for a suitable partner in a daughter's marriage.

> *"Yeah, Hmong and Americans are different. Like, in the American culture you can fall in love and then you can get married. But in the Hmong culture, your family, your parents, help you to find a good husband. Personally, I want to get married to someone I fall in love with, not someone my mom and dad pick out for me to marry. People should be able to fall in love before they get married. I don't think my parents understand this. I don't think they know this is what I want."*

Of the twelve pre-adult Hmong that were interviewed for this research, eleven were unmarried. These teens shared that they frequently felt their parents misunderstood them and they showed little interest in Hmong traditions and culture. This group of young Hmong identified more strongly with their perceptions of life in America and the American culture.

This fifteen-year-old Hmong female shared the sentiments of many of the pre-adult Hmong that were interviewed for this study. Her desires to act like and do things like an American teenager are frequently in direct conflict with her parent's wishes. These differences have created miscommunications and distinctive cultural gaps within her family unit.

> *"Sometimes my parents don't understand me. They want me to do things that I don't want to do. They want us kids to go along with Hmong culture and stuff like that, and I don't always like to do it. I*

*want to do stuff with my friends and my parents
will say no. Like, I want to go to my friend's house
and stuff and they don't want me to go. They just
don't understand why this is so important to me.
Like, I want to wear American clothes and stuff
that the other kids are wearing in school. I try to
do some of the Hmong things, but I feel like I have
more American culture inside me. Because I don't
talk so much in Hmong and I am not good at it. I
feel Hmong, but I like to do American things."*

This young adult Hmong father describes the communication gaps he
sees developing between his son and himself because of their different
levels of adaptation to the United States. He believes it is inevitable that
his son will become more American.

*"My children, yeah, they are more American than
me. I can tell my son sometimes to do something
and he doesn't do what I say. He has his own
mind. In Laos, there is no question that a child
listens to his father. So, sooner or later he is
going to be speaking more in English than in
Hmong. I try my best to teach him the Hmong
ways, but I know he will go more to American
ways."*

The Hmong parents that participated in this study were frequently
resigned to their children losing many of the Hmong traditions and fully
expected that their younger children would become more like Americans.
Despite this resignation expressed by many of the Hmong who were
parents of young children, they worried about their children and how the
differences between the two cultures would effect core values and beliefs.

Although the families had made the decision to relocate into the United
States, there was a reported sense of loss as parents longed for the Hmong
basic core values which were familiar and comforting to them particularly
in a time of great change and adaptation.

A older adult female Hmong shared in the interview that her younger
children would become more Americanized because they were being raised
in the United States and have little exposure or understanding of the
Hmong life in Laos.

"My oldest children, they are all like Hmong. The youngest children, they are not so good with this. They are becoming more and more like Americans. I think this is so because they live here and not so much they live in Laos or Thailand. They are more like Americans, because they know this life and no other. I don't think there is anything to be done about this. They are here now and this is the way it will be."

This sense of resignation was shared by many of the older adult Hmong that were interviewed. The desire for their children and grandchildren to succeed in the United States of America was viewed as more important than an understanding and appreciation for the Hmong life and traditions. Despite this process of letting go and allowing their children to become more Americanized, basic values of respect and hard work were emphasized by all of the older adult Hmong interviewed.

All of the older adult Hmong participants believed that if their children held the basic values of respect and hard work as important, the parent was indeed a success in passing on the Hmong culture.

A 76-year-old Hmong male believed that it is important for his children and grandchildren to adjust to a new life in the United States of America and to become more like Americans. This older adult Hmong also emphasized the importance of respecting one's elders and working hard to succeed in life.

"Our children and our grandchildren are speaking in English now. They know more about this country than we do. I am happy that my children know English and that they are Christians. These are good things and important things to living in the United States. They need to find jobs and work and pay bills. They need to live like American people do. I only wish they are respectful and work hard. I am more concerned with this than if my children can speak in Hmong or know about Hmong things."

All of the Hmong participants that had children reported during the interviews that their children were well behaved or good. This was expressed despite the communication problems faced in most of the families between parents and children.

This 68-year-old Hmong male recognized that his children will become more Americanized. He sees this as a natural occurrence. This older adult Hmong is willing to accept this change, knowing that this can further divide intergenerational relationships. He expressed a hope to instill the value of respect for elders in his children, which he shared, will help in bridging the communication and generation gaps experienced within his family.

> *"My children are good children. They listen to their parents and we don't have any problems in this way. They are becoming more like Americans now, but they still know to respect Their parents. We expect them to become more like Americans because they live here now and so they should. The main thing is that they should always be respectful to their parents. Sometimes it is a problem for us that they think and act more like Americans, but we know they still respect us and this is what is most important to us."*

Many of the pre-adult Hmong and their younger siblings that were raised in the United States of America bear the responsibility of serving as the family cultural broker and translator. A fifteen-year-old Hmong female shared how she carries this responsibility of serving the needs of her family to communicate with the outside world. She carries a great responsibility on her shoulders as she handles a number of family transactions within the American community. On one occasion, when this researcher was observing this family in their home, the fifteen-year-old female was filling out a home loan application for her older brother and his wife. Problems faced with non-Hmong neighbors and discussions with law enforcement have all been handled for the family by this fifteen-year-old. She describes the difficulties she has experienced from trying to function in and negotiate between two different cultures.

> *"Well, I think that everyone is counting on me. I take them places and go places with them because I speak the best English. I feel like I am supposed to be like the little Angel here. Because I speak and understand English the*

best. I try to live in both American and Hmong,
you know? Sometimes my parents are acting
really weird like when I am in American dress.
Like bell bottoms and stuff are popular in
school, but my mom wants me to wear regular
pants and my mom, she keeps saying stuff like
that's now how we want you to dress and stuff.
When I am home, I try to dress like my mom
wants me to and when I am in school, I try to
dress like my friends so I fit in and stuff."

This younger adult male Hmong, age 31, is currently separated from his Cambodian wife and has no extended family living in the immediate area. He raises his five young children alone. He sees the changing relationship between himself and his children as inevitable. He views his parents as persons that are frozen in a time that no longer exists. His decision to marry a non-Hmong person was a personal statement that stemmed from his own beliefs that life is different for the Hmong living in the United States.

"It is very hard here because no matter what,
the children will be and need to be more
Americanized. You cannot stop this from
happening. No matter what you try to do or to
say, it won't change this fact one bit. Kids
think that the ways of their parents are too old
fashioned and they don't want to do things the
old way. Like my parents, they were in a time
that became frozen for them, to them, life stayed
the same as it was in Laos. Even though when
they came here, it was different. It was like they
woke up in a time period that was ahead of them
and they didn't know what to do about it. They
knew a lot about life, but they didn't know a lot
about America. My parents grew up in a small
village where everyone is the same and life stays
the same for centuries. So, they were narrow in
their thinking when they came here. They didn't
know there is different points of view and they
wanted their children to speak in Hmong."

This younger adult Hmong male went on to share his views on the cultural changes that have occurred among second and third generation Hmong born in the United States of America. His thoughts on how American children are raised show distinctive differences from child rearing in the country of Laos.

> *"...But the kids, they think the parents ways are silly. We see that other people talk in English, and wear different clothes. We want to be like American kids, which is natural for kids to want to do. In this country, it is wonderful for kids, because they have all kinds of freedoms. Kids can say whatever they want to their parents and the parents can do nothing about it. Parents in this country even listen to their kids! In Laos, a parent would never do such a thing. Kids here get a good education and they get confidence in themselves and the kids use this against their parents to get more independence and freedoms."*

The Hmong participants discussed the role changes within the families that occurred since relocating to the United States of America. Hmong women now work outside the home and many function as head of the household due to their husband's inability to work or absence from the home. A 58-year-old Hmong female described how her relationship with her husband and her children is different since moving to the United States.

> *"My husband and I, well, our relationship is different now. Here in the U.S., I am working and I would not be working in Laos. We share everything, the house and car payment. We have a joint bank account. We work together to raise our children. We had to change when we moved to this country, but we still respect each other. Even my children are now equal to each other. My daughters go to school alongside their brothers. They are equal in getting an education. They can make their own minds in this country and don't always have to listen to the words of their parents."*

The younger adult Hmong participants were more likely to embrace the changes in family relationships that occurred as a result of relocating to the United States of America. The younger married Hmong adults perceived that the success of a family resulted in the achievements of both the husband and the wife.

This 21-year-old Hmong male expressed his feelings about his relationship with his wife as an equal partnership, distinctly different from what their relationship would be like in Laos. He viewed these changes as an opportunity for both husband and wife to succeed.

> *"Well, I don't know if conflict is the right word to use. But our relationship is different than what it would be if we were in Laos. Husband and wife are equal people in this country and now my wife is equal to me. We help each other in this country. If we were in Laos or Thailand, my wife would have to listen to what I say. She would not have her own free mind. This is not conflict really, it is just different. I want my wife to do well. I want her to go to school and to help the family to have a better life. I think this is a good thing in the U.S. that we are equal to each other and help each other."*

A number of the younger adult Hmong with children had made a conscious decision to give their children American names. This decision was based on the logic that their children would spend the remainder of their lives in the United States of America and would need to embrace and fit into the American way of life.

This 21-year-old Hmong male discussed how his relationship with his daughter will be different than it would have been if she were born in Laos. His views are similar to many of the other younger adult Hmong that were interviewed, in that he accepts that his children will become more American than their parents or grandparents.

> *"My children are more American now. They need to do this so they can have a better life here. The old Hmong ways will not help them when they go to look for jobs and try to make*

a family life here. I think many Hmong families will have more problems because sometimes the parents don't understand their children. But I think this is needed because the children must become more American. My daughter will be more American than she will Hmong. I have even named her an American name. This will help her to make life easier in this country. "

Prejudice

The Hmong participants for this study shared a number of experiences where others perceived their differences in a negative light. Prejudice is a learned behavior that is a unsubstantiated judgment or opinion about an individual or a group, either favorable or unfavorable. However, the term most often denotes an unfavorable or antagonistic attitude toward other people based on their membership in another social or ethnic group. A distinctive characteristic of prejudice is that it relies on stereotypes or generalizations about the group against which the prejudice is directed (Encarta on-line, 2002).

The differences between groups of people can result in examining members of another group as strangers or outsiders. Most people are generally attracted to those who are similar in background and share certain life experiences.

Most of the Hmong families that were interviewed for this research did not define negative or prejudicial experiences as mistreatment by Americans, but instead reported that they felt they were not welcome in their community by neighbors and co-workers. This was frequently cited as a sense or a perception, more than actual encounters. This researcher does not mean in any way to diminish actual experiences that occur due to racism or prejudice. On the contrary, several of the Hmong participants expressed experiencing actual hate crimes.

This research merely points out that the majority of the Hmong persons interviewed for this particular study discussed their experiences with prejudice more in terms of feelings and perceptions, rather than actual negative encounters with people in their community. This may actually be the result of a low incidence of hate crimes against the Hmong in Rochester, or it may be because the Hmong interviewed were reluctant to share these experiences with a Euro-American researcher.

This 60-year-old Hmong male shared his frustrations from his inability to understand why someone who doesn't even know him may not like him.

> *"Some people are very good and some people are not liking us. The people who are good to us, I really want to talk to them, but I cannot speak English. The people who do not like me, I cannot speak to them either. For this, I am very glad, because they are people that I don't want to talk to. I don't know if they have anything good to say to me, and I don't understand them."*

The pre-adult Hmong interviewed for this study frequently held a different view from the younger adult and adult Hmong participants. Although many of the younger Hmong related stories of negative comments that were made by their peers in school, these were often perceived not so much as racist remarks, but as a form of teasing or initiation.

This fifteen-year-old Hmong female shares her perceptions on this subject. She believes that her classmates who had made racist comments about her were actually teasing and perceived this as an opportunity to make new friends rather than a threat.

> *"Oh, sometimes kids say something, but I think they are teasing me. I don't like it, but I think if they will be my friends, they are just teasing. Like when I first came to school here, they called me stupid and said things like, 'Why don't you learn English, you are stupid.' Things like that. But I think they are just joking around and don't really mean what they are saying."*

Some of the Hmong participants were able to share negative experiences they had where racial comments were overheard. This 68-year-old Hmong male described a personal encounter at a gas station where the clerk was hostile when taking his money for gasoline.

*"Sometimes I see it in people's eyes. They look
at you with such hatred in their eyes. They will
say things to me like 'Why don't you go home.'
'Why don't you go spend your own money.'
You know these people hate you and there is
nothing you can do about it to change their
mind."*

Several of the Hmong persons interviewed had experienced more
frequent negative encounters in the Rochester community than others. The
most reported incidence of prejudice experienced by these Hmong
participants was with neighbors. Three families (20 percent) reported
having hostile encounters with neighbors. All three of these Hmong
families had retained their traditional Hmong religion.

These three Hmong families related the negative encounters with
neighbors because they had too many children and the children made too
much noise. All of these three families that had retained their traditional
Hmong religion expressed the downside as their religious practices and
rituals could be quite noisy. This was an acceptable practice in Laos where
neighbors did not live so close together, or practiced the same religious
rituals, whereas those same religious rituals and practices were uncommon
and even unacceptable by some people in the United States of America.

This 61-year-old Hmong female discussed her thoughts on prejudice and
dealing with neighbors who are displeased with sharing the community
with Hmong people.

*"Our neighbor has taken eggs to our house and
our car. He doesn't like us and wishes we
would move away. Americans have a very easy
face, you can read their thoughts. They look at
you with such hate and you know that they are
against you, not as a person, but because you
are different, you are not white."*

The pre-adult Hmong participants frequently expressed having
experiences at school with classmates that were unfriendly or hostile.
These experiences were usually placed upon the Hmong child when first
arriving in a new school, where the other children would ridicule them
because of the Hmong child's limited English speaking abilities. Most of
the pre-adult Hmong subjects reported these types of encounters
diminishing over time, as they acclimated to their new school.

This fourteen-year-old Hmong male shared during the interview his experiences with mistreatment from fellow classmates in school and his response to the mistreatment.

> *"Some kids in school will say things like, 'Why don't you go back where you come from." They will tell you that you don't belong here or call you a FOB [Fresh Off the Boat]. I don't care what they say. I don't want to get into trouble at school, so I just walk away from them."*

Several of the younger adult Hmong interviewed, expressed experiences with negative encounters at their work place. A 26-year-old Hmong male shared his perceptions that his colleagues at work just did not like him. He expressed fear of retaliation as a reason not to tell his employer of his experiences with harassment. A 31-year-old Hmong male shared his observations that his employer paid immigrant employees less money and that opportunities for career advancement were less likely to occur for the Hmong.

> *"This is just my personal opinion, but, I think I am not treated equally to the white workers. I think the white workers make more money than me. I work hard and I am in the company longer, but new white workers come and they get paid more money than me. So I know this is truth and that I am not being treated equally."*

REFERENCES

Encarta On-Line (2002). [online]. Available: http://encarta.msn.com/reference.

Chapter 13

Analysis of Migration Experience

The Hmong have never had an official homeland of their own, and as a people, they have experienced numerous migrations prior to coming to the United States of America. These migrations have continually redefined aspects of the Hmong culture, despite the fact that culture is central to the Hmong way of life. The following Hmong proverb adeptly expresses the adaptability of the Hmong as a people.

> *"Hla dej yuav hle khau,*
> *Tsiv teb tsaws chaw yuav hle hau."*

This translates to:

> *"Cross the river, you take off your shoes,*
> *Flee from the country, you'll take off your status."*

> *(Yang, 1993).*

Regardless of the Hmong's historically adaptable view on migration, this process can be so disruptive to families that it can add an entire extra stage to the life cycle and to those members who must negotiate the stress of such dramatic cultural changes and experiences.

Adjusting to a new culture is not a singular event, but a prolonged developmental process that affects each family member differently, depending on their phase of personal development in the life cycle process.

This is noted in the views that were shared by the Hmong persons interviewed for this study as their perceptions of life in the United States of America were different based on their ages and gender.

The younger adult and pre-adult Hmong participants were much more likely to embrace the cultural differences of living in the United States. Older adult Hmong were less likely to do so. For the older adult Hmong participants, the problems of adjustment to life in the United States of America were so overwhelming, that many had physical and mental impairments that were largely untreated because of cultural and traditional views about medical treatment and health care.

The Hmong, who had immigrated to the United States of America as children or as young adults, had the greater interest and potential for adaptation to the American culture in terms of educational opportunities, careers, and marriage. They were also more vulnerable to losing specific components of the family's cultural traditions and heritage.

Families that migrated with younger children were often more fortunate because of their ability to provide support to one and other, but were more vulnerable to role changes as the older adult Hmong became increasingly more dependent on younger family members to serve as cultural brokers and translators in order to negotiate goods and services from the outside community.

The older adult Hmong refugees were more likely to acculturate at a much slower pace than their children and grandchildren, which resulted in dramatic changes in the power structure of the family. Older adult Hmong were likely to have little or minimal decision making abilities while their children would serve as interpreters to the new culture for the family. As a result, leadership became threatened, as children were left without effective adult authority to support them, and without a positive ethnic identity to ease their adaptation to life in a new culture.

The experience of migration in later life has been especially difficult for the older adult Hmong as they leave behind entire life experiences as well as social and cultural resources. The Hmong elders were predominately non-English speaking, which helped to further their isolation and deprived them of socialization and formal and informal community support systems. The older adult Hmong frequently have relied solely on other family members for socialization, support, and to negotiate services within the host culture.

Older adult Hmong who are fortunate to live in ethnically rich neighborhoods, such as those elderly Hmong who reside in St. Paul or Minneapolis, Minnesota, may be able to postpone some of the stress associated with adjustment to their new host culture. These older adult Hmong are able to remain in an environment where there are others who speak the same language, share the same foods, and practice the same traditions, rituals, and holidays.

Regardless of whether additional support is available or not, eventually the Hmong family will have to face intergenerational conflicts as their children and grandchildren become more accustomed to life in the new culture and reject the old values and traditions of their ancestors. Intergenerational conflict is inevitable and often reflects the value struggles of the Hmong families as they adapt to life in the new culture.

Chapter 14

Theme Four – Religion

Traditional Hmong and Christian Practices

The Hmong subjects interviewed for this research went from a country were their religion was acceptable and customary, to living in the United States of America, where their traditional practices of Animism were clearly in the minority. Religious practices, holidays, and traditions now took on a new and different meaning and importance for the Hmong.

For many of the Hmong participants in this study, it was easier to abandon their traditional Hmong religion and adopt the beliefs and practices of Christianity. This author hesitates to suggest that these Hmong persons have totally abandoned their religious and spiritual beliefs, and in fact, this author suspects that for many of the Hmong persons interviewed for this research, these traditional beliefs were in fact retained, but suppressed.

An example of this is in the way the Hmong participants handled matters related to deceased loved ones. Funeral rituals and practices generally stem from one's religious background and beliefs. There was no exception found with the Hmong participants interviewed for this research. A 55-year-old Hmong male participant indicated his family, for all practical purposes, was Christian. The family held membership in a local Baptist Church. However, for a recently deceased family member, it was clear that rituals and traditions were very important in the burial process.

> "The burial place is most important. It must be on a
> hill or in a high position, be in a good environment,
> with good soil and good trees. Around the hill
> should be beautiful. We believe that if a person is
> buried in a good place, on a hill and beautiful
> with trees and good soil, that person will come
> back to help the younger people, so they can get
> a good education, they can have a good job or
> even be a king! This is why it is so important to
> find the right place to bury the dead."

This older adult Hmong male may have recognized that this belief was in contradiction with Christian burial practices, because he went on to share that he believes this selection process for land use is a common practice by many Americans in the United States.

> "Umm, I believe that the American people do the
> same as the Hmong people do. I know that the
> American people do the same thing because I went
> to Washington, D.C., and I saw the White House
> and it is in a good location, a good and powerful
> place. Some very important people found this
> place, because I can tell that they know what they
> are doing when they build the White House on
> that spot."

The challenges of practicing traditional Hmong religion in the United States was intensified for the small numbers of Hmong who retained these values and beliefs, as many of their fellow Hmong had abandoned and now disapproved of these traditional practices.

Religion and its practices played a prominent theme with all of the Hmong families that participated in this study. Sixty percent of the Hmong families, or nine out of the fifteen families (60 percent) interviewed state their religion as Baptist. All of these families converted to Christianity after moving to the United States of America. Six of the nine families (67 percent) received their United States sponsorship from the same local area Baptist Church.

Of the remaining six Hmong families in this study, three of the families (20 percent) were Catholic. These three Hmong families reported during the interview process that their families had converted to Catholicism several generations prior while still residing in Laos. The final three

Hmong families (20 percent) that were interviewed reported maintaining their traditional Hmong religion, a religion that is based in Animism.

During the Asian Wars, economic upheaval and military invasions broadened the possibilities for some of the Hmong families who began to identify with the native people of Laos in their dress and politics. Lao was the language of education for a small percentage of people. Particularly those that converted to Christianity were more likely to have educational opportunities within the country.

One of the Hmong families reported being Catholic for the past four generations. This family's decision to convert to Catholicism occurred while still residing in the country of Laos. This 50-year-old Hmong female shared during the interview process that despite her family entering the United States as Christians, there were differences that were noticed between Catholics in Laos and Catholics in the United States. This was due to ethnic differences in interpretation and the practices of Catholicism from two very different countries.

> *"Since my family was in Laos, we were Catholic. So we would go to the Catholic Church and have Catholic ways. The customs and cultures are different in Laos than in here. We are long time Catholics and I don't remember who in my family ever did the older Hmong religion. We always go to the Catholic Church for a long time now. But even because my children are Catholic, they still keep some Hmong ways. I don't have a problem to discipline my children. They are older and do what I ask them to do. They have respect for their mother."*

Another Hmong family that had been Catholic prior to coming to the United States reported that the conversion to Catholicism took place two generations ago in Laos. This 26-year-old Hmong male believes that his father may have converted to Catholicism in order to prepare his family for an eventual move from the country of Laos. As a result of this religious conversion, the traditional Hmong religious practices are completely lost to this family.

> *"My father converted to Catholic religion I think, when he was very young age. I was always a Catholic. I don't know anything about the Hmong religion because I never learned about it. My father never told me*

*about it. We don't ever follow the Hmong religion in
my family, we always follow the Catholic religion.
When we came to the United States, we asked our
Priest in Thailand about Catholic Church in Rochester.
Our Priest in Thailand knew this Priest in Rochester
and he told us to come to this Catholic Church, so we
go there now.*"

Those Hmong families that converted to Christianity upon arrival to the
United States of America, frequently cited their conversion as a way of
helping their children to adapt to the new host culture. This 25-year-old
Hmong male believed that his children would fair better in the United
States of America if they were Christians.

*"My children will be Christians. I think they need
to know about it so they can talk to different people
and understand the American culture. Otherwise,
the people they talk to won't understand them.*"

One of the Hmong families that was sponsored by a local Baptist Church
to come to the United States of American spoke of how the church offered
assistance to them while the family was still in a Thai refugee camp. This
church offered help to a number of Hmong families in the Rochester
community and currently offers mass services in the Hmong language to
many of the local community Hmong. This older adult Hmong male
reported a sense of indebtedness and deep gratitude to the Baptist Church
for bringing his family to the United States and converted to Christianity in
an obligatory gesture.

*"The church helped me and my family when we
needed help. They helped us with money when we
needed it. I think that they expect that we are
Christian and that we will go to their church.
Without this, they won't speak to us anymore.
We are not in our homeland anymore, and they
want us to change everything.*"

This sense of obligation to convert to Christianity was expressed by
many of the Hmong families that participated in this research. A majority
of the families likened their conversion to an informal or unspoken

pressure, most frequently received from other Hmong families that were members of a Christian Church.

This older adult female Hmong was a Shaman for most of her adult life in Laos, now at 74 years of age, she shared during an interview her experiences in converting to Christianity. Because of her strong ties to the traditional Hmong religion, as a prior spiritual guide and healer, this older adult Hmong female experienced a great deal of inner turmoil, internal distress, and anxiety as she attempted to shed her traditional beliefs and in a sense, deserted her spiritual ancestors. The internal conflicts faced by this older adult Hmong female as a result of her religious conversion had resulted in the need for medical attention and ultimately the consumption of tranquilizers and anti-anxiety medications in order to purge herself of the "hauntings" she experiences from her spiritual ancestors.

> *"We converted to Christianity because we want to have a religion and we cannot have our religion here. When I became a Christian, it was very hard for me. In my country, I was a Shaman, and so when I became a Christian, I had to give up my work as a Shaman. Our Minister at our church said to me that I have to do this, so I must do as he said. For a long time, the Spirits of my Ancestors would come to me and call on me, wanting to know why I stopped being a Shaman. I had to tell them to go away and leave me alone. It was very hard, but I could not do anything about it."*

A number of the Hmong families that were interviewed for this study had difficulty expressing their reasons for converting to the Christian faith. This researcher believes most of the Hmong participants had experienced some type of informal pressure or a sense of obligation to convert, because of the assistance their families received from the local churches.

A 34-year-old Hmong male shared his decision to change from the traditional Hmong religion to Christianity as a means of helping his family to adjust to life in the United States of America. His decision was based on his belief of how difficult it would be for his children to practice the traditional Hmong religion in the United States.

> *"We are Christians. I became a Christian once I arrived here. My children are raised to be Christians. This is more important than the*

Hmong religion. Christian is very different
from the Hmong religion. We are now separate
from these people. My children won't know
anything about this old religion. I think that it
is best that we are now Baptist. We did this
because we know it is best to be a Christian
in this country. It is the right thing to do
because we are living in the United States
now. I want my children to have a better life
in this country and to go to church to be
where other people are."

Several of the Hmong participants repeatedly shared similar sentiments as the older adult Hmong male above. The sense of obligation to a Christian church was further illustrated by the comments of an older adult Hmong female, aged 58 years, as she related how the Baptist Church helped her family upon their arrival to Rochester by locating an affordable place for them to live.

"We are very fortunate. The Baptist Church
found us this house. They got us this house, but
no cooking pots, no furniture, no clothes. We
had only a bare house, but we had a house!
The old customs are lost in this country, they
are better forgotten. It is best to become a
Christian and a United States Citizen."

The Hmong families in this study that chose to retain their traditional Hmong religious beliefs were in the minority. This created a sense of further alienation from not only the majority culture, but from those Hmong who made the conscious decision to convert to Christianity. This 60-year-old Hmong male shared his observations of the division between the Hmong of Rochester who are now Christian and those Hmong who retained their old religion.

"I never went to a church in my life. Some Hmong
are now Christians and they don't talk to us
anymore. They get angry at us that we are not
Christian too. They don't talk to us or invite us in
their homes. Lots of people want us to become
Christians but we don't want to do this."

Many of the Hmong subjects from this study who had retained their traditional religious beliefs expressed how difficult it was to practice their religion within their own homes. This older adult Hmong female, aged 49, believed that there was a distinctive pressure by the majority community to abandon old Hmong religious beliefs and to convert to Christianity. She shared how difficult it was for her family to practice the act of animal sacrifice, an important part of Hmong religion, in the United States of America.

> *"You Americans, you want us to become Christian. Then the Hmong who become Christians, their lives become much easier. It is so important for us to keep our religion. But many Hmong will convert because their lives become much easier when they are Christians. We have problems with our religion here because in this country, you cannot sacrifice in your home, but this is our belief. We don't want to convert because we are not Christians."*

The Hmong families within this study that wished to continue with traditional Hmong religious practices recognized that conversion to Christianity would certainly make their lives in the United States of America that much easier. However, these Hmong families felt a deep sense of commitment to their traditions, heritage, and religion. This 26-year-old Hmong female shared her opinion on the pressures felt by many Hmong to convert to Christianity.

> *"We don't want to become Christians. But we know a lot of Hmong who are now Christian. They want us to become Christian too. But we don't want to do this. There is a lot of pressure to become a Christian. Other Hmong people will ask us why didn't we become Christians. They think just because we live in America, we should do this. I think that we learn our religion from generation to generation and that others think we don't have enough knowledge here to practice it anymore."*

Chapter 15

Analysis of Religion

Religion plays a significant role for all cultures and for many people. The significance of religion to the Hmong is certainly no exception. Throughout history and well into the present day, many ethnic groups have been persecuted for their religious beliefs, as in the case of the Jewish people who maintained a sense of cultural and religious identity despite anti-Semitism throughout world history.

For many ethnic groups, religion is a method of coping with the pressures of adjustment to a new society (Gelfand and Fandetti, 1986). The results of how religion plays an important role in coping within a new society is clearly illustrated by the example of the Shaman mentioned in Chapter Fourteen who converted to Christianity.

This Shaman's decision to convert to Christianity was clearly for the perceived benefits of her family, yet her personal convictions created great inner turmoil resulting in a psychological breakdown that presented with auditory and visual hallucinations. The distress from this inner conflict resulted in the need for this female Shaman to take anti-depressant and anti-anxiety medications, which had lessened the hallucinations to a certain extent. However, she had continued to complain of a host of physical ailments such as headaches, chronic neck pain, backaches, and insomnia, which were not easily treated by her general practitioner.

Common beliefs and shared experiences are the basis for an ethnic group's sense of community. A religious community helps to preserve and transmit beliefs, symbols, rituals, and literature that are culturally meaningful and significant to the believer. Common beliefs and traditions lead to a wealth of cultural norms within a religious community regarding such matters as one's diet, holy days, art, music, politics, birth, death, marriage and how to lead a good life.

The Hmong in this study who were able to identify with a religious community shared common beliefs, stories, and vocabulary. Words within one's personal religion may contain communal and significant meanings or references that other groups who are not a part of that religious order do not share.

The Hmong families within this research who retained their traditional Hmong religion reported a greater sense of family satisfaction, less intergenerational conflicts, and a better acceptance of the cultural changes that their children would ultimately take on as a result of moving to the United States of America.

This older adult Hmong male is a practicing Shaman in Rochester, Minnesota. During an interview, he stressed the importance of the Hmong being able to adapt to life in the United States.

> *"Yes, our children are becoming more like Americans, but they still respect their parents. We expect that our children will become more like Americans, this is how it should be, because now they live here. The important thing is that we teach them to show respect."*

Spirituality is the "general human experience of developing a sense of meaning, purpose, and morality (Canda, 1988). In contrast to spirituality, organized religion encompasses the formal beliefs and practices that are held in common with others.

Often, one's religious beliefs evolve within a particular religious group and involve an affiliation with a religious organization such as a church, mosque or temple. While formal religion and spirituality and interrelated, they are also separate phenomena. People can and do raise spiritual questions about the meaning of life that are outside their prescribed religious order.

Theologian and philosopher, Paul Tillich (1959), presented a concept of religion that encompasses both the pluralism of religion and spirituality. Tillich believed that religion provides the depth in all life's functions, rather than just a special function or component of one's spiritual side. He used the metaphor "depth" to mean that the religious aspect points to that which is ultimate, infinite and unconditional in a person's spiritual life.

Tillich believed religion was neither a system of beliefs or an institution. Instead, he believed that religion points to the presence of the infinite in every finite expression of human life.

Spirituality is fundamental in defining how each of us will attribute purpose and meaning to life, death, and how we should live day to day.

The answers to these spiritual questions of life and death affect whether we feel hopeful or hopeless about our existence.

Religious and spiritual convictions ultimately determine the directions we will take when we reach turning points in our lives, permeate our relationships with other people, help us to make moral and ethical decisions, and connect us to the rest of humanity. Spirituality shapes how we view ourselves and other people, how we perceive problems and how we define solutions. Spirituality defines our sense of responsibility, feelings of guilt, obligations to others, and interpretations of justice and fairness.

The Hmong participants from this study that had converted to Christianity upon arrival to the United States of America expressed a greater sense of dissatisfaction with their religious beliefs. The decision to convert to Christianity was not based on a fundamental belief in one God or a specific religion, but rather was a choice of convenience in order to "fit" into their new community and as a sense of obligation or duty to those who helped the family to migrate and ultimately to survive within the United States.

Most of the Hmong families that had converted to Christianity upon arrival in the United States of America attended church sporadically and did not expect their children to attend at all. This was evident in the majority of the Hmong participants who were interviewed sharing that they were indeed Christians, but did not attend church on a regular basis.

The Hmong worldview of animism and shamanism are beliefs that involve animal sacrifices to spirits of animate and inanimate objects as well as spirits of nature. This religious conviction is considerably different from the American majority that practices religions involving one God, or the convictions held by modern day science and technology.

Shamanism and animism define the worldview of what it means to be a Hmong person. Hmong beliefs in shamanism and animism have accompanying traditional practices that come into direct conflict with American health and safety codes. Many Hmong persons living in the United States of America depend on Shamans to perform ritual healing and other significant life event ceremonies.

Shaman are responsible for burial of family members and loved ones, animal sacrifices, births, marriages and other key events in the lives of the Hmong. Misunderstandings between traditional Hmong beliefs and practices and the United States health, funeral, and law enforcement codes create spiritual crises for the Hmong as religious practices are physical manifestations of their belief system and what makes a Hmong person.

An example of this dilemma was noted in the Minneapolis Star Tribune (March 19, 2000). A practicing Shaman in Hugo, Minnesota a rural community just north of St. Paul and Minneapolis was asked by local community officials to cease sacrificial practices on his farm. The city of Hugo claimed that the Shaman's farm violated city zoning ordinances. The city of Hugo took their complaint to the courts. Further, the Minnesota Department of Agriculture threatened to shut down the farm in April of 2000. Neighbors close to the farm complained about the traffic, improper disposal of manure and animal carcasses, runoff of bloody water, sounds of dying animals, and the smell of burning hair.

The Shaman filed a countersuit against the city of Hugo. He claimed that the city was discriminatory against his business because it draws Asian and African immigrants whose religious and cultural needs are misunderstood. Hugo city officials claimed the issue was about proper land usage and not about culture. However at that time, the city of Hugo did not have specific regulations against the operation of a "slaughterhouse."

These conflicts between the United States health and safety codes and the traditional Hmong religion result in many traditional Hmong families practicing limited and revised versions of their traditional Hmong religion. Sacrifices are frequently kept to a minimum and held in secrecy. Spiritual healing is done with the express permission of neighbors, due to the noise level, or it is practiced in locations where it would not be viewed as disruptive to others.

In this study, the Hmong participants that continued to practice their traditional Hmong religion had reported experiencing greater conflicts with their non-Hmong neighbors who disapproved of the "congregational" meetings and noise levels in the Hmong homes.

REFERENCES

Canda, C. R., (1988). Spirituality, Religious Diversity, and Social Work Practice. *Social Casework.* 69. pp. 238-247.

Gelfand, D., and Fandetti, D., (1986). The Emergent Nature of Ethnicity: Dilemmas in Assessment. *Social Casework.* 67. pp. 542-550.

Slaughterhouse Dispute. (2000, March 19). Minneapolis Star Tribune. B1.

Tillich, P., (1959). *Theology of Culture.* New York City, NY: Oxford University Press.

Chapter 16

Discussion of Themes

As noted throughout the findings and analysis chapters of the various themes, the acculturation levels of the Hmong participants in this study varied within and between family members. Cultural awareness was measured by the Hmong participant's ability to communicate in English, opportunities for and levels of education, opportunities in and integration of employment, understanding and use of health care, roles and responsibilities of family members, and the ability to understand and negotiate within the new host community.

Ethnic loyalty was measured within this study by the Hmong participant's understanding and ability to communicate in the Hmong language, perceptions and practices within Hmong traditions and rituals, and the roles and responsibilities of family members.

Non-voluntary migration experience was examined by the Hmong participant's coping abilities and strategies and the stress resulting from experiences related in the Asian Wars, multi-migration experiences as a refugee in Thailand and in the United States of America, and the perceptions and experiences with prejudice as a refugee in the United States.

A final component that was examined after completion of the interviews was the effect religion and conversion to Christianity has had on the Hmong refugees. This component involved examining perceptions of the Hmongs pressures to convert and the problems experienced by Hmong families who continued to practice traditional Hmong religion.

The findings of this study indicate differences in cultural awareness and ethnic loyalty between the older and younger adult Hmong and the pre-adult Hmong that participated in this study. Older adult Hmong were more likely to view their migration to the United States of America as an involuntary decision based on their experiences from living in a war-torn country. The older adult Hmong overwhelmingly reported during the interview process a desire to return to live in Laos. Not the Laos as it currently exists, but the country of Laos as remembered in their past. The older adult Hmongs desire was to return to the lives that the Hmong were used to living while residing in that country.

Younger adult and pre-adult Hmong participants expressed less of an interest in returning the country of Laos. Those younger adult Hmong who had memories of the country of Laos expressed some regrets at having to leave their homeland, but clearly expressed an interest in remaining in the United States because of the availability of education and job opportunities.

The pre-adult Hmong participants interviewed had no recollection of their family's life in Laos. Some of the pre-adult Hmong had memories of their lives in Thailand and actually expressed a stronger identification with the country of Thailand. The pre-adult Hmong participants for this study did not consider their families' migration to the United States of America as a non-voluntary act. Rather, they viewed their families move to the United States as an opportunity for family success and survival.

The Hmong participants' perceptions of the host Anglo culture varied based on the Hmong subject's prior personal experiences with the Anglo culture. Those who were old enough to remember the Asian Wars and their forced evacuation from Laos into Thailand and subsequently long stays within refugee camps had different perceptions of Anglo culture than the younger Hmong subjects who did not have these experiences.

The older adult Hmong who were interviewed for this study relied almost exclusively on younger family members to serve as their translators and culture brokers within their new host community. These older adult Hmong had limited understanding of the American culture and their host community. Their restricted English speaking abilities created a constant barrier to their new community and the environment surrounding them.

The older adult Hmong were more apt to view their host culture as a hostile environment where they were forced to adapt and change their cultural values and beliefs. An example of this is the older adult Hmongs view of their legal rights in the United States of America. Overwhelmingly, older adult Hmong viewed the American legal system in opposition to traditional Hmong patriarchal family structure. Older adult Hmong reported feeling they had no right to discipline and ultimately control their children. They believed that in the United States, their children were granted more rights than the parents. The fear of being turned in by their own children for imposing disciplinary measures was quite prevalent. Older adult Hmong parents believed their children could have them arrested for child abuse should they have required the children to follow traditional Hmong family roles.

The Hmong participants for this study, particularly older adult Hmong, have experienced considerable socio-cultural dissonance (Chau, 1989), from the stress of belonging to two distinctly different and opposing cultures, Hmong and American. The need to draw on family and culture for support has become increasingly important for the Rochester area Hmong community as differences in status and culture, unfamiliarity with the American culture, experiences with prejudice and restricted access to services such as medical care has created isolation for many of the older adult Hmong in the community.

Younger adult Hmong showed a much greater understanding of the host Anglo culture, but expressed a desire to find a healthy balance between their traditional Hmong and their new American cultures. Conflicts between the two cultures were often considered burdensome for the younger adult Hmong as they sought ways to have a sense of continuity within their families and seek resolution to socio-cultural dissonance among family members.

The younger adult Hmong participants expressed the importance of keeping key elements of the Hmong culture within their lives. These key elements included things such as the Hmong language and the Hmong New Year as a method of passing on the Hmong culture and identity to their children.

The pre-adult Hmong participants showed a much greater understanding of the American culture and a willingness to adopt American values and beliefs. These pre-adult Hmong expressed very little desire or willingness to continue with the traditional Hmong culture and what traditional practices they did maintain were more out of a sense of obligation to their family and the older adult members.

The Hmong New Year, was believed by the older adult and younger adult Hmong participants as the greatest opportunity for Rochester area Hmong to retain their culture and traditions. A Hmong New Year celebration is held each December at the Olmsted County Fairgrounds. This was noted by all of the older adult and younger adult Hmong participants as one of the most important things they could do to retain their cultural identity.

The pre-adult Hmong participants were less enthusiastic about the Hmong New Year celebration. Those pre-adult Hmong subjects that would attend the New Year events reported doing so out of a sense of duty and responsibility to their family. Some of the pre-adult Hmong participants blatantly defied their families and refused to attend the Hmong New Year celebration. The majority of pre-adult Hmong participants did not find the Hmong New Year to be an important or necessary event in their lives.

The Hmong participants for this study showed a high degree of discrepancy between the acculturation levels of older, younger, and pre-adult Hmong. This discrepancy created acculturation gaps, which were related to the younger adult and pre-adult Hmong's increased identification with the American culture and their decreased identification with their family's culture of origin. This shift created family difficulties, disharmony, discord, and communication gaps within and between family members.

REFERENCES

Chau, K., (1989). Sociocultural Dissonance Among Ethnic Minority Populations. *Social Casework* 70. pp 224-239.

Chapter 17

Member Checking

On April 7, 2000, a focus group was held with four Rochester area Hmong persons who were participants for this research. The purpose of this focus group was to discuss the content, findings and recommendations resulting from this research. All the Hmong families who participated in this project were invited to attend the focus group. Three of the fifteen families were represented at the focus group meeting.

Interestingly, the Hmong participants who attended the focus group were all males in their mid to late 20's and served within their families as translator and cultural broker with the outside host environment. The purpose of the focus group meeting was to share insights and analysis of the findings as well as seek the feedback from the Hmong participants.

Several findings that were discussed in the focus group are worth reiterating. The members most frequently discussed these findings at the focus group meeting. All the members of the focus group believed that the findings accurately reflected the Hmong population in Rochester and believed that Hmong in other cities across the United States experienced similar situations and problems. The focus groups clarification and affirmation to the themes presented within this research gave more confidence to the conclusions.

The focus group believed that immigration, voluntary or non-voluntary, was not an easy process. With the decision to leave behind their homeland, the Hmong had sacrificed much of their ethnic identity and what it meant to be a Hmong person. This was particularly noted in the loss of identity found in many families with younger children that no longer identified with their country or culture of origin.

The tragic aspects of immigration experienced by all the Hmong within this study included leaving family members behind and loss of status, identity and security, particularly for many of the older adult Hmong. This sense of identity, status and security was sacrificed and the Hmong found themselves in a new, strange, and unknown country with cultural norms and rules that did not fit with the traditional Hmong way of life. The fact that many of the Hmong experienced a drop in their social status upon arrival to the United States of America demonstrates how some of their fears regarding migration were based in reality.

Benefits of Immigration

The benefits brought on by immigration expressed by the members of the focus group were that the United States of America was truly a land of opportunity for many. The group believed that these opportunities were a benefit for the Hmong children and their futures. The group believed access to education was readily available to all persons and that job possibilities were endless.

The group shared that they believed the older adult Hmong family members were willing to sacrifice their lives for the sake of their children. These sacrifices included the elderly working in factories, as janitors and maids, and in other low paying jobs. The focus group members believed that the older adult Hmong carried a significant burden in providing for the financial needs of their families, and had sacrificed their own hopes and dreams for a better life so that their children could have greater opportunities.

All of the members of the focus group stressed the importance of religion and how it played a key role in the Hmong of Rochester in their development of relationships and alliances with other Hmong. The focus group expressed that they found the majority of Hmong who had converted to Christianity since residing in the United States, did so out of a sense of responsibility and obligation to their American benefactors. It was also noted that the Hmong of Rochester who had converted to Christianity frequently had done so as a matter of convenience. The perception of the focus group members was that those who are Christian in the United States of America have an easier time locating the goods and services necessary to survival.

Two of the focus group members shared that some Hmong had converted to Christianity and became members of a local Baptist Church in order to have the opportunity to meet and socialize with other Hmong. These two focus group members believed that the church served as a public meeting place for socialization among families and as an opportunity for elders to meet and discuss Hmong issues.

All of the focus group members believed that the older adult Hmong of Rochester used components of both the traditional Hmong religion and Christianity in their daily lives. An example that was given was that most older adult Hmong still believe that illnesses are caused by evil spirits, but that the elderly will most likely pray to God instead of seeking help from a Shaman or by sacrificing an animal.

All of the members of the focus group expressed their concerns for the older adult Hmong of Rochester and how to address health issues, particularly undiagnosed or untreated Depression and Post-Traumatic Stress Disorder. The focus group members stated that they were pleased to hear that a non-Hmong person was able to spend time with the local Rochester area Hmong families and note these health issues as real problems for the elderly. As a group, the members said they wanted to seek out practical ways of helping their elder Hmong in dealing with these and other health related problems.

The Hmong person that was used as a translator during this research is now working as a Mental Health Case Manager in the Rochester community. Discussion from the focus group members evolved around the possibility of this individual offering an Older Adult Hmong Support Group to allow the elders an opportunity to share their experiences and feelings about life in the United States of America in a comfortable forum.

The focus group members also expressed an interest in providing younger Hmong generations with information about the history and traditions of the Hmong people. The group discussed serving as guest lecturers and presenters in middle and high school classrooms to educate younger Hmong and non-Hmong children about the Hmong culture.

The focus group members believed that it would be beneficial to share the history of the Hmong religion to younger children, regardless of whether their family practiced traditional Hmong religion or Christianity. The members of the focus group believed that the Hmong religion was an important and rich part of the Hmong culture and traditions. Sharing the history and traditions of this religion with younger Hmong would be another way of helping the young learn about their Hmong heritage.

Chapter 18

Conclusion and Recommendations

Summary

This research study was designed to investigate one of the newest refugee groups to arrive in the Midwestern United States, the Hmong refugees from Laos and Thailand. This research study focused on how multigenerational Hmong families were adapting to life in the city of Rochester, Minnesota.

The method of data collection for this research study was qualitative interviewing through in-depth individual interviews and through participant observation. Participants for the research study were recruited through purposeful sampling, volunteering, and snowball sampling techniques. Criteria for inclusion in this research study were: 1. Being Hmong; 2. Resident of Rochester, Minnesota and; 3. Being at least 13 years of age or older. Grounded theory methodology was the primary tool for data analysis.

The preceding findings were meant to create a present day picture of the lives of the Hmong residents of Rochester, Minnesota through their process of adaptation and acculturation. Their stories illuminate the reality of their individual and family experiences and the impact of many of the older adult Hmongs' survival from war, life in refugee camps, and eventual migration to the United States of America.

The findings presented clearly demonstrate that the Hmong subjects interviewed for this research study showed a high degree of discrepancy between acculturation levels based on age and country of origin at time of migration. This discrepancy has created an acculturation gap which is related to the older Hmong's continued ties to Hmong culture, traditions, and way of life, whereas, the younger Hmong showed increased identification with the American culture and a decreased identification with their family's culture of origin. This shift created changes in the family power structure, increased family misunderstandings, miscommunications, and other related difficulties, and gaps in language spoken between intergenerational family members.

Edmonston and Passel (1994), noted that the process of integration takes several generations, and varies across families and dimensions of families. An example of this is how quickly second and third generation Hmong family members acquired English skills compared to the first generation Hmong family members.

Structural and broader social integration was noted in the third generation of Hmong families as these members struggled to become more accepted in the mainstream American culture and became less concerned with the traditional Hmong culture.

Hynie (1997), also presented the issues of acculturation in family based terms. As noted in his work, the family is the central unit for most immigrant and refugee family dynamics. The family plays a significant role in the interplay of individual, interpersonal, and inter-group development of relationships. The Hmong families that participated in this study have been trying to negotiate their lives from two opposing cultures. The younger Hmong of the second and third generations are acculturating at a much more rapid pace than their older, first generation Hmong members. As Hynie indicates, these family dynamics are representative of a microcosm of both the conflicts and the processes by which adaptation defines the experience of immigrants.

Zamichow (1992), had noted that the uprooting of established values and exposure to a new culture creates various types of psychological distress, including cultural shock, social alienation, psychological conflict, psychosomatic symptoms and post-traumatic stress. This psychological distress and related symptoms were evident in the older adult Hmong that were interviewed for this research study. The American culture is quite different from what many of the older adult Hmong were used to when living in an agricultural society with limited educational and job opportunities. Health problems by these older adult Hmong participants were displayed most predominantly as headaches, stomachaches, insomnia, excessive worry, and stress, all of which can be attributed to a form of psychological distress and cultural shock.

Post Study Questionnaire

A post study questionnaire was completed within two weeks of conclusion of the interviews conducted for this research study. The Hmong individual who served as translator during the data collection phase of this research study completed post study questionnaires in personal interviews. The results of the post study questionnaire provided the following data:

Table 18.1

Post Study Questionnaire

Question	Yes	No
The interviewer explained the purpose of this research to me.	36	1
The interviewer treated me fairly.	37	0
I was comfortable with the interview process.	35	2
I was comfortable with the questions asked of me.	35	2
I was able to refrain from answering questions that I did not feel comfortable answering.	36	1
I would recommend additional participants for this study.	36	1
I feel comfortable that my confidentiality will be respected in this study.	37	0

Three of the thirty-seven Hmong respondents requested a copy of the results from this research study upon completion. Additional comments on the post study questionnaire were as follows:

"It was very nice talking with you."
"It was nice to get to know you."
"This is a nice project."
"It was nice to have you in our home."
"It is nice you are doing this project."
"Everything went very well."
"It was very nice to know you."
"This was a fine interview."
"Rank the questions by number instead of yes or no."
"Good project."
"All went very well."
"Nice to meet you."
"You did a great job interviewing me."
"It was nice to know you and see that you care about Hmong."

Conclusions

This research study was designed to answer the question: *What effect does non-voluntary migration have on the acculturation levels as measured by cultural awareness and ethnic loyalty.* The findings demonstrate that there is a difference in the understanding of non-voluntary migration between the age groups that were interviewed.

The older adult Hmong clearly considered their having to leave Laos as a non-voluntary act and would have preferred to remain in their homeland. Young adult Hmong were less likely to view their migration to the United States of America as non-voluntary. Rather, this was a decision based on an understanding that their families would not be able to return to Laos and that living in Thailand in refugee camps was a temporary and transitional living situation. The pre-adult Hmong viewed themselves as Americans first and Hmong second. They did not view their families move to the United States of America as a non-voluntary act rather, the decision to come to America was for the perceived benefit of all family members.

Awareness of the American culture was found to be less significant in the older Adult Hmong who were unable to identify with the United States as their new homeland. The older adult Hmong expressed more interest in their children adapting to the American culture. This view was based on an understanding that their children would need to make their lives within the United States of America.

The younger adult Hmong were found to harbor a more middle ground. They were acutely aware of their host culture, but not necessarily accepting of it. The younger adult Hmong held the perception that they had a strong responsibility to serve as translators and cultural brokers for their families. Serving as translators and negotiators of goods and services within their new host culture, the younger adult Hmong sought ways to keep their Hmong culture alive, while trying to assist their families in receiving the maximum benefits of their new environment.

The pre-adult Hmong participants were more likely to be aware of and identify with the American culture. This group viewed much of the traditional Hmong ways as irrelevant to their lives in the United States of America. The pre-adult Hmong viewed themselves as Americans and as such wanted to adopt the American culture, values, beliefs, and way of life.

Older adult Hmong participants held most strongly to loyalty for their ethnic culture. They believed that the Hmong culture, values, and beliefs helped to maintain a healthy balance in their marriages and their families. However, the older adult Hmong were willing to allow their children and grandchildren be more "like Americans", as long as the younger Hmong generations in their families were willing to abide by certain rules. These rules included: respect for elders, following the example and authority of older males and the eldest sons within the family, working hard and providing for the entire family, and marriage to other Hmong, in particular, those Hmong who were chosen by the parents as compatible.

Younger adult Hmong expressed an interest in maintaining parts of the Hmong culture within their families. The areas of Hmong culture considered most important by younger adult Hmong participants were respect for elders, understanding of the history of the Hmong people, and attendance at the Hmong New Year celebration.

Pre-adult Hmong expressed the least interest in loyalty to the Hmong culture. Hmong values that were considered the most important to the pre-adult Hmong participants were respect for one's parents. This age group expressed reluctance in the need to understand Hmong history and traditions, as well as the importance of attending the Hmong New Year celebration.

Intergenerational conflict within the Hmong families occurred most frequently in the areas of ethnic loyalty and cultural awareness. Older adult Hmong participants shared their frustrations during the interview process in getting their younger children to listen to them, as well as in getting younger Hmong children interested in the Hmong culture and history.

The pre-adult Hmong participants shared their frustrations during the interview process in getting their parents to understand the need to be like their American peers, to find suitable members of the opposite sex to date or marry, to wear American clothes and express their individuality and freedom of choice. These pre-adult Hmong participants stressed the importance of an older sibling in serving as a negotiator with their parents, and as such, had a great deal of respect for their older siblings.

Younger adult Hmong were most frequently serving as the go-between with their parents and younger siblings or children. Serving as translators and negotiators for what would be considered acceptable behavior for the younger Hmong children, as well as seeking compromise between intergenerational family members, in an effort to restore family harmony and peace.

The additional question of how do the Hmong perceive their host Anglo culture produced varied responses that are presented again by the age of the Hmong participants interviewed.

The older adult Hmong perceived American culture as imposing of certain values that were in direct conflict with the Hmong culture and values. Conflict was most prevalent in how the older adult Hmong participants perceived they could discipline their children. Older adult Hmong believed that American culture denied them the right to impose disciplinary measures against disobedient children. This perception went further in that the older adult Hmong participants expressed concerns that in the American culture, their children could have them arrested for even the slightest attempt on the parent's part to impose household rules.

Younger adult Hmong had a far different understanding of the American culture compared to their elders. The younger adult Hmong participants perceived the American culture as being rich in opportunities for education, employment and job promotions, and greatr equality in marriage and family relationships.

The pre-adult Hmong participants showed the greatest interest in the American culture and expressed their perceptions of the American cultural system as having greater opportunities for education and work possibilities, as well as the ability to marry whom one chooses, express one's own religious preferences, live where one wishes to live, and express one's opinions freely.

In regard to the question of how the Hmong adjust to the American social systems, the older adult Hmong participants were found most likely to have difficulties with adjustment. This was best expressed by the older adult Hmong participants reports of high stress levels as they worried about paying their bills, working at menial jobs, lack of understanding and access to medical and dental care, and the ability to communicate with others in their community.

The younger adult Hmong participants faired much better in their adjustment to live in the United States of America. Although it was noted that the younger adult Hmong experienced high stress levels as they attempted to serve as mediators and negotiators within their own families.

The pre-adult Hmong participants were the most likely to express an easy transition and adjustment to the American culture and way of life. The pre-adult Hmong subjects were more likely to identify with the American culture and to abandon their Hmong culture.

The question of how much do the Hmong learn about their new environment is directly related to the education levels of the participants in this research study. The older adult Hmong had little or no formal education. They were unable to communicate in the English language and as a result, relied solely on their younger adult and pre-adult aged children to interpret and negotiate with the host environment.

Younger adult and pre-adult Hmong participants had the opportunity to receive some or all of their formal education within the United States of America. These two groups expressed the greatest comfort levels in their ability to communicate in the English language. The younger adult and pre-adult Hmong participants shared during the interview process that they had learned about their host environment through the public school system and by their interactions with others in the community.

The last question asked in this research study was how the Hmong retain traditions within the American culture. Overwhelmingly, in all families, this was done through the celebration of the Hmong New Year and through the sharing of the Hmong language.

The dimension of religion was presented as a separate theme in this study as a number of the Hmong participants had converted to Christianity upon their arrival to the United States of America. The conversion to Christianity was noted more as a sense of obligation and responsibility because of the assistance provided by some Christian churches to the Hmong refugees. The Hmong conversion to Christianity was more likely due to a sense of obligation than it was to changes in their religious beliefs.

The loss of traditional Hmong religion in the majority of the Hmong families interviewed was found to create a new tension within the family units and with individual members. This tension extended to outside Hmong families, clans, and tribes as a distinctive division between Christian and non-Christian alliances was formed.

Recommendations

The findings presented in this study on acculturation of refugees are not necessarily new or surprising. The acculturation levels of the Hmong participants interviewed for this study are well within the findings of many research studies completed on refugees and immigrants. However, there are several interesting and unique dimensions that are presented within this study, which leave the door open for additional research in this area.

First is the concept of religion and the conversion to Christianity by some of the Hmong refugees. The loss of traditional Hmong religion in many of the subjects interviewed presented a deep sense of loss and a considerable amount of tension among extended families, clans and tribes.

Loss was expressed by many of the Hmong participants in their sense of mourning and longing for traditional religious convictions, the inability to pass this religion on to future Hmong generations and the inability to pay religious respect to one's elders and ancestors. Tensions resulted from the division between families, clans, and tribes. Those Hmong persons who had converted versus those Hmong persons who had retained their traditional religion. The Hmong families from this study who had chosen to retain their traditional religion expressed feeling a great deal of pressure from the Christian Hmong members to convert. Further, many of these subjects reported receiving pressure from their non-Hmong neighbors to cease in doing their traditional religious rituals and practices within the home.

A suggested area for more in-depth study would be to further examine the issue of religion within the Hmong culture. How does conversion to Christianity affect acculturation levels as perceived by ethnic loyalty and cultural awareness? Additional questions would be: 1. How does the conversion to Christianity affect Hmong family relationships? 2. How does conversion to Christianity affect relationships between Hmong families and clans, particularly with those Hmong families that have chosen not to convert and maintain their traditional religious practices?

Helping professionals need to be sensitive to the issues important to Hmong families when working with them on intergenerational and adjustment issues. In terms of how the helping professional might be useful in cross-cultural misunderstandings within refugee families, Smith, Tobin, Tchabo, and Power (1995), suggest three clinical considerations that are specific to this type of work.

First, ensure that the helping professional is fully informed regarding the specific ethnic norms of the families they are working with. This may seem obvious to some helping professionals, but if the professional does not understand the cultural nuances of the Hmong people, it would be wise to seek the consultation of a professional who does.

Second, pay particular attention to the engagement process of the helping relationship. This is especially important for the Hmong refugees, as their views of the dominant culture are colored with their experiences of discrimination, impoverishment, and alienation. These issues certainly effect the engagement process as relationship building and trust will take more time to achieve, particularly if the helping professional working with the family is non-Hmong.

Third, the helping professional should take on the role of cultural broker when working with the Hmong refugee family. In so doing, the professional goes back and forth between the positions of ethnic loyalty and cultural awareness or adaptation, establishing the validity and importance of each within the helping process.

Helping professionals who work with the Hmong refugee family need to seek ways in which both cultural awareness and ethnic loyalty can be intertwined and integrated within the family's working systems. This integration of both components will help the Hmong refugee family rather than force them into a position of having to pick one method of problem solving over another or force assimilation and adaptation unto the Hmong family.

References

Edmonston, B., and Passel, J.S., (1994). *Immigration and Ethnicity: The Integration of America's Newest Arrivals.* Washington, DC: The Urban Institute Press.

Hynie, M., (1997). *From Conflict to Compromise: Immigrant Families and the Processes of Acculturation.* Montreal, Canada: McGill University Press.

Smith, G., Tobin, S., Tchabo, E., and Power, P., (1995). *Strengthening Aging Families: Diversity in Practice and Policy.* Thousand Oaks, CA: Sage Publications.

Zamichow, N., *No Way to Escape Fear.* (1992, February 10). The Los Angeles Times. B1-B3.

Appendix A

Interview Guide

Demographic Data

1. How many members reside in your home?

___ 1 ___ 2-3 ___ 4-5 ___ 6-7 ___ 8-9 ___ 10 or more

2. What are the ages and gender of the persons residing in your home?

___ 0-4	___ M	___ F	___ 5-9	___ M	___ F
___ 10-14	___ M	___ F	___ 15-19	___ M	___ F
___ 20-29	___ M	___ F	___ 30-39	___ M	___ F
___ 40-49	___ M	___ F	___ 50-59	___ M	___ F
___ 60-69	___ M	___ F	___ 70-79	___ M	___ F
___ 80 and over	___ M	___ F			

3. How long has your family resided in the United States?

___ Less than one year ___ 1-3 years ___ 4-6 years
___ 7-10 years ___ 11-15 years ___ 15 years or more

4. How long has your family resided in this region of the United States?

___ Less than one year ___ 1-3 years ___ 4-6 years
___ 7-10 years ___ 11-15 years ___ 15 years or more

5. What was your family's first U.S. destination city?_____

6. How long did you live in that city?_____

7. Were there other cities in the U.S. that you have lived in?

Where?_____ How Long?_____

8. When did your family move to Rochester, Minnesota?_____

9. Was there a particular reason why you moved to Rochester?_____

10. What is your family's country of origin?

___ Laos   ___ Thailand   ___Cambodia   ___Vietnam   ___China
Other _____

11. What is your family's clan of origin?

12. What other states in the U.S. has your family resided before moving to
    Minnesota? _____

13. What other countries has your family residing in after leaving your
    country of origin?_____

14. What is your current status in the U.S.?

___ Temporary Resident   ___ Permanent Resident   ___ U.S. Citizen
___ Other _____

15. Does another family member currently sponsor you? _____

16. Who sponsored you? _____

Housing

17. Do you or members of your household have any difficulties locating
    suitable housing? _____

18. Do you or members of your household have difficulties in the
    neighborhood you currently live in? _____

19. Do you or members of your household have difficulty with the cost of your housing?

20. Do you or members of your household live in overcrowded housing conditions? (e.g. more tenants than allowed by the landlord)

21. Do you or members of your household live in poor housing conditions? (e.g. electrical, plumbing, sanitation problems)

22. What type of housing is your current residence?

___House ___ Apartment ___Dormitory ___Single Room
___Trailer ___ Other

23. Are you renting or buying your residence? ___ Rent ___ Buying

24. How much is your monthly rent or mortgage payment?

___ $0-249 ___ $250-399 ___ $400-549 ___$550-699
___ $700-849 ___ $850-999 ___ $1000-1149 ___ $1150 or up

Income

25. What is your total take home household income per month?

___ $0-249 ___ $250-499 ___ $500-749 ___ $750-999
___ $1000-1249 ___ $1250-1499 ___ $1500-1749 ___ $1750 or up

26. What are your sources of income?

___ Employment ___ SSI ___ SSA ___ Savings ___ Sponsor
___ GA ___ Other _____

27. Do you have enough income to meet your monthly expenses?_____

Employment

28. Do you or members of your household have any difficulty locating employment? _____

29. Are there members of your household currently unemployed and looking for work? _____

30. Are you or others in your household satisfied/dissatisfied with your current employment? _____

31. Are you or others in your household underemployed? (e.g. working at a level below your qualifications)

32. Do you or others in your household have insufficient job skills? ____

33. Do you or others in your household have difficulty accessing necessary job skill training? (e.g. language barrier, cost, transportation, accessibility) _____

Language

34. What is the first language you learned to speak? _____

35. What language was spoken in your home when you were a child? ___

36. What language are you most comfortable speaking in now? _____

37. In your opinion, how well do you understand spoken English? _____

38. In your opinion, how well do you speak English? _____

39. In your opinion, how well do you read English? _____

40. In your opinion, how well do you write English? _____

41. What language do you usually speak with your spouse, children, or other members of your household? _____

42. What language do you usually speak at family gatherings? _____

43. What language do you usually speak with your friends? _____

44. What language do you usually speak with your neighbors? _____

45. What language do you usually speak with people at work or at school?

46. In what language are the television programs or video movies that you watch? _____

47. In what language are the radio programs you listen to? _____

48. In what language are the books and magazines you read? _____

Family

49. Do you or members of your family have any difficulties relating to your family life now? _____

50. Do you or members of your family have any difficulties being separated from family members in another location? _____

51. What is the relationship to this family member and where are they currently located? _____

52. Do you or members of your family have any difficulties locating family members in another location? _____

53. Which family members are missing and when were they last seen? __

54. Do you or members of your family have a fear in communicating your feelings to family and friends in your country of origin? _____

55. Do you or members of your family experience any conflict between husband and wife over each other's role in the family due to a change in culture? _____

56. Do you or members of your family experience any conflict concerning children learning the American cultural values and not accepting the Hmong cultural values? _____

57. Do you or members of your family have any difficulties maintaining family customs in the United States? _____

58. Do you or members of your family experience any conflicts between relatives living together in the same household? _____

Health

59. Do you or any members of your family have any health-related problems?

Family Member _____ Health Problem _____

60. Has this family member sought the advice of a medical doctor or health care practitioner for this health problem? _____

61. Do you or any members of your family experience stress or stress related illnesses? (e.g. headaches, stomachaches, fatigue)

Family Member _____ Health Problem _____

62. Has this family member sought the advice of a medical doctor or health care practitioner for this problem? _____

63. Are you or any members of your family experiencing homesickness?

Family Member: _____

64. Do you or any members of your family experience painful memories of war and departure from your homeland?

Family Member: _____

65. Has this family member sought the help of a mental health professional for this problem? _____

66. Do you or any members of your family use alcohol or other drugs?

Family Member: _____ Type of Use:_____
Frequency of Use: _____

67. Do you or any members of your family experience difficulties in getting medical care? _____

68. Do you or any members of your family experience difficulties in getting dental care? _____

69. Do you or members of your family experience difficulties in getting vision care? _____

70. Do you or members of your family experience difficulties in getting hospital care? _____

71. Do you or members of your family experience difficulties in getting prescription medications? _____

72. Do you or members of your family experience difficulties in getting mental health care? _____

73. Do you or any members of your family have medical insurance coverage?

Family Member: _____ Type of Coverage: _____

Preservation of Culture

74. In your opinion, how well do the children in your household understand the history of the Hmong? _____

75. Who in the family is the person responsible for sharing the family and Hmong history to the children?
_____

76. In your opinion, how well do the children in your household follow the Hmong culture and ways of life? _____

77. Who in the family is the person responsible for sharing Hmong culture and traditions with the children? _____

78. How important do you feel it is for the children in your household to celebrate Hmong holidays and rituals? _____

79. Who in the family is the person responsible for organizing the family members on Hmong holidays and for Hmong rituals? _____

80. In your opinion, how important do you feel it is for the children in your household to maintain Hmong religious beliefs? _____

81. Who in the family is the person responsible for teaching Hmong religious beliefs to others in the household? _____

82. Do you or members of your family attend a local church or place of worship?

Family Member: _____ Church: _____

Education, Community, and Social Environment

83. Do you or members of your household experience any difficulties adjusting to American life? _____

84. Do you or members of your household feel you have inferior social status as a refugee? _____

85. Do you or members of your household experience prejudice against refugees? Can you give an example of prejudice that has occurred against you or members of your family? _____

86. Do you or members of your household experience difficulties in practicing your own religion? _____

87. Do you or other members of your household feel you are expected to practice Christian religion? _____

88. Do you or others in your household experience difficulty in locating appropriate burial places for deceased family members? _____

89. Do you or others in your household have difficulty expressing yourself to Americans due to language or cultural barriers? _____

90. Do you or others in your household have difficulty understanding Americans due to language or cultural barriers? _____

91. Do you or others in your household have difficulty with transportation? _____

92. Does anyone in your family own an automobile?

Family Member: _____

93. Do you or another person in your household have a valid state driver's license? _____

94. Do the family members who own a vehicle carry automobile insurance?

_____

95. In your opinion, do you or other members of your household have educational opportunities available to you? _____

96. Are the children in your household experiencing any school-related problems? _____

97. Are you or other members of your household receiving English language training? _____

98. Are there enough English classes available in the community for you and your family? _____

99. Are you satisfied with the English classes you and your family are receiving? (e.g. Have you learned sufficient English skills to communicate in your community)

100. Do you read newspapers, magazines and books in your own language?

101. Are you able to locate newspapers, magazines, and books in your own language? _____

102. Do you read newspapers, magazines and books in English? _____

Nutrition

103. Do you or members of your household have any concerns about a healthy diet?

104. Has a medical doctor or health care practitioner suggested a diet change for any members of your family due to a health problem? ____

105. Do you or your family have any difficulties locating the foods native to your culture? _____

106.Do you or any members of your household know to prepare different types of American foods? _____

Traditional Family Structure

107.Does your family keep in close contact with extended family members? _____

108.In your opinion, how important is it that brothers have responsibility to protect their sisters? _____

109.In your opinion, how important is it that sisters have the obligation to respect their brother's authority? _____

110.In your opinion, should grown children live wherever they want to or should they live close to their parents so that they can help each other?

111.In your opinion, if the father is absent, who should make the most important decisions for the family? _____

Information Access

112.Does any member of your family have a checking account? _____

113.Does any member of your family have the responsibility to balance the checking account? _____

114.Does any member of your family have a savings account? _____

115.Does any member of your family possess credit cards? _____

116.Does any member of your family have the responsibility to prepare a monthly budget? _____

117.Does any member of your family currently invest money? _____ Type of Investments: _____

118. Does any member of your family know how to prepare Federal and State Tax Returns? _____

119.Have any members of your family purchased a home? _____

120. Do any members of your family understand and use insurance coverage? _____ Type of Coverage: _____

121. Are any members of your family currently trying to acquire a driver's license? _____

122. Are there any members of your household who are able to drive but unable to pass the written driver's license examination due to lack of necessary English skills? _____

123. Are there any members of your family who possess an automobile and know how to maintain the vehicle? _____

124. Are there any members of your family who plan to or have already financed an automobile? _____

125. Do members of your household who drive understand the local traffic laws? _____

126. Have any members of your household received traffic violations in the past five years? _____

127. Do you and members of your household understand the American legal system? _____

128. Do you or members of your household experience any difficulties in the operation of household equipment? _____

129. Do you or members of your household experience problems in the appropriate storage of foods? _____

130. Does any member of your household currently take prescription medications? _____ Type: _____

131. Does any member of your household who takes prescription medications have difficulties taking the medications as prescribed?

132. Does any member of your household who takes prescription medications have questions about the medications purpose?

133.Does any member of your household currently take over the counter medications? _____ Types:_____

134.Did the member of your household who takes over the counter medications consult a pharmacist or medical practitioner on the uses of the medication? _____

135.Does the member of your household who takes over the counter medications understand how to take them (according to package directions)? _____

136.Do you or any members of your household currently take herbal remedies? _____ Types: _____

137.Did the members of your household taking herbal remedies consult a herbalist or natural healer on the uses of this remedy? _____

138.Did the members of your household taking herbal remedies have an understanding on how to take the medication? _____

139. Do you or other members of your household take vitamin or mineral supplements? _____ Types: _____

140.Did the members of your household who take vitamin or mineral supplements consult a health care practitioner on how to take the supplement? _____

141.Do you or members of your family use infant formulas or infant foods? _____ Type: _____

142.Did the family members who prepare infant formulas or infant foods consult with a health care practitioner on the uses of these products?

143.Does the family members who prepare infant formulas and infant foods understand the product uses? _____

144.Does the members of your household have clothing appropriate for Minnesota seasonal weather?

145.Do you or members of your family know how to care for different types of clothing?

Appendix B

Informed Consent Form

Title of the Study: Migration of the Hmong to the Midwestern United States

1. I agree to be asked a series of questions about my residential status in Rochester, Minnesota and how I have adjusted to life in the United States.
2. These questions will be asked in Rochester, Minnesota and will take about three hours to complete.
3. The purpose of asking these questions is to better understand how the Hmong people have adjusted to life in Rochester, Minnesota and what acculturation areas of need currently are unmet.
4. I understand that some of the questions might be difficult to answer. The researcher has explained that my name will not be recorded on the questionnaire and that my answers will be used only for the purpose of analyzing the data.
5. I understand that this research may result in the development of future social services for Hmong residing in Rochester, Minnesota and may not be of immediate value to my personally.
6. I understand that I can refuse to answer any question and can withdraw from this study without jeopardizing my standing in receiving future possible benefits that may be developed as a result of this study.
7. I am not receiving any compensation for participating in this study.

Signature: _____ Date: _____

Appendix C

Participant Guide

Thank you for agreeing to participate in this interview. The purpose of this study is to examine recollections of the Hmong in Rochester, Minnesota and their migration to Minnesota. This study will help to build a knowledge base about Hmong as refugees in the United States of America and their needs related to adapting to life in Minnesota.

This study will be used to form strategies to respond to the Rochester area Hmong needs and find ways to assist Hmong in becoming active members of their new community.

As a participant in this study, you will be asked a series of questions. A Hmong translator will be available to assist those participants who have difficulties communicating in the English language. This interview will take approximately three hours to complete. Each member of your family over the age of 13 years will be asked if they are willing to participate. Each individual family member has the right to decide whether or not he or she wishes to participate and permission of parents or authorized guardian will be sought before interviewing minor children.

As a participant in this study, you are not required to answer any questions that you do not wish to answer. Your name will be excluded in the final written research to protect your identity. The final research may be published sometime in the future.

In approximately two weeks after your interview, a Hmong speaking person will contact you in person to ask you a few questions about your experiences in this interview. Your answers will be confidential and your name will not be used in any comments you provide. Your answers in no way effect your ability to receive future services or benefits that may occur as a result of this research. If you wish, you may request a copy of the results of this study when it is completed.

Appendix D

Hmong Study Post Questionnaire

Your participation in the research project concerning the Migration of Hmong to the Midwestern United States is greatly appreciated. Please take a few moments now to answer the following questions concerning the interview process and how you were treated during the interview. You do not have to place your name on this questionnaire. Thank you.

1. The interviewer thoroughly explained the purpose of this research to me.
___ Yes   ___ No

2. The interviewer treated me fairly.
___ Yes   ___ No

3. I was comfortable during the interview process.
___ Yes   ___ No

4. I was comfortable with the questions asked of me.
___ Yes   ___ No

5. I was able to refrain from answering questions that I did not feel comfortable answering.
___ Yes   ___ No

6. I would recommend additional participants for this study.
___ Yes   ___ No

7. I feel comfortable that my confidentiality will be respected in this
    study.
    ___ Yes   ___ No

8. Additional Comments or Suggestions: _____

_____

_____

■■

This section may be detached from the above questionnaire if you wish to
have your answers remain anonymous. Use this section to request a copy
of the results of this completed study.

Name: _____

Address:_____

Appendix E

List of Codes and Number of Occurrences

Code	Frequency	Lines
Cultural Awareness	67	274
Adjustments	133	568
Appliances	36	42
Diet	50	124
Infant Formula	20	25
Locating Hmong Food	37	54
Medical Reasons to Change	28	31
Preparing American Foods	43	111
Storage	35	38
Driver's License	66	104
Acquiring	70	108
Tickets or Accidents	30	40
Traffic Laws	31	35
Legal System	40	84
Transportation	46	77
Automobile	44	67
Insurance	15	21
Maintenance	36	51
Weather and Clothing	37	86
Wash and Care	37	50
Banking	16	21
Budgeting	49	60
Checking	18	24
Credit Cards	15	33
Investments	13	26

Code	Frequency	Lines
Savings	15	28
Education	171	438
Difficulties	69	223
English as Second Language	72	105
English Language	98	214
Comfort Level	25	52
Learning English	49	89
Reading	77	176
Speaking	135	276
Understanding	94	206
Writing	39	60
Health	84	200
Dental Care	38	80
Diet	37	68
Insurance	69	116
Medical Care	124	234
Medications	52	103
Herbal	38	50
How to Take	30	36
Over the Counter	38	46
How to Take	33	37
Prescription	84	118
How to Take	39	46
Vitamins	15	17
How to Take	6	6
Mental Health Care	66	93
Vision Care	38	69
Housing	56	161
Locating Housing	35	108
Type of Residence	35	61
Condition	42	126
Cost	56	97
Neighborhood	87	248
Ownership	36	50
People in Residence	27	67
Income	47	95

Code	Frequency	Lines
Employment	123	226
Difficulties	54	147
Unemployment	16	28
Locating	50	115
Income Sources	41	83
Monthly Income	37	70
Insurance	36	45
Monthly Expenses	38	72
Taxes	15	16
Prejudice	77	323
Refugee Status	68	294
Demographics	30	60
Ages	15	44
Gender	15	44
Country of Origin	37	50
Clan	37	48
Length in United States	24	45
Other Cities	34	68
Years in Rochester	41	63
Reasons for Living In	19	72
Other Countries of Residence	19	37
United States Destination	20	30
United States Status	42	75
Sponsor	21	61
Ethnic Preservation	169	553
Children and	138	406
Hmong Customs	79	178
Hmong History	74	135
Hmong Holidays	74	142
Hmong Religion	106	283
Children's Responsibility	116	343
Brothers	48	141
Sisters	43	127
Contact with Extended Family	95	204
Locating	42	96
Family	153	547
Family Customs	41	164
Family Relationships	137	487
Family Separations	76	220

Code	Frequency	Lines
Homesickness	47	132
Family Stress	62	211
Post Traumatic Stress	15	115
Alcohol and Drug Usage	35	42
War	46	241
Husband and Wife	62	186
Parents and Children	194	587
Friends	40	108
Head of Household	45	120
Hmong Burial	35	94
Hmong Food	29	50
Hmong Language	120	227
Other Languages	44	91
Reading	78	160
Speaking	98	176
Writing	32	72

Author Index

Author Index

Subject Index

Subject Index